MW01613755

Radio-TV
Newswriting

A Workbook

Radio-TV
Newswriting

A Workbook

K. TIM WULFEMEYER

IOWA STATE UNIVERSITY PRESS / AMES

K. Tim Wulfemeyer is professor in the School of Communication at San Diego State University. He has degrees from Fullerton College, San Diego State University, Iowa State University and the University of California at Los Angeles. He has worked as a writer, reporter, producer, photojournalist, news announcer and sports announcer for radio and television stations in California, Iowa, New Mexico, Texas and Hawaii. He has taught journalism at universities in Iowa, New Mexico, California and Hawaii. Wulfemeyer has written three journalism textbooks, 25 research journal articles and 40 research papers that were presented during meetings of professional journalists or journalism educators.

© 1995 Iowa State University Press, Ames, Iowa 50014
All rights reserved

Authorization to photocopy items for internal or personal use, or the internal or personal use of specific clients, is granted by Iowa State University Press, provided that the base fee of $.10 per copy is paid directly to the Copyright Clearance Center, 27 Congress Street, Salem, MA 01970. For those organizations that have been granted a photocopy license by CCC, a separate system of payments has been arranged. The fee code for users of the Transactional Reporting Service is 0-8138-0747-6/95 $.10.

∞ Printed on acid-free paper in the United States of America

First edition, 1995

Library of Congress Cataloging-in-Publication Data

Wulfemeyer, K. Tim
    Radio-TV newswriting: a workbook / K. Tim Wulfemeyer.—
1st ed.
        p.   cm.
    ISBN 0-8138-0747-6 (acid-free paper)
    1. Broadcast journalism—Authorship—Handbooks, manuals,
etc. 2. Radio journalism. 3. Television broadcasting of news.
I. Title
PN4784.B75W82   1995
808'.06067—dc20   95-12194

Last digit is the print number: 9 8 7 6 5 4 3 2

Contents

Introduction

Writing news for a radio or television station is different from writing news for the print media. Listeners or viewers don't get a written version of a story, so radio-TV news copy must be written in a way that will help audience members understand complex issues and events the first time they hear and/or see them.

Radio-TV news must be written in a simple, direct manner. It must be written so a newscaster can read the copy easily and communicate effectively to people who often are not giving the newscaster their full attention.

One of the keys to effective radio-TV newswriting is the ability to write the way people talk in their everyday conversations. Radio-TV newswriters must strive to achieve an informal, conversational, flowing writing style. Ideally, newscasters should sound as if they're simply talking about issues and events with friends rather than reading news copy to a faceless mass of strangers.

The information, examples and exercises in this workbook are designed to help you begin to develop your knowledge, skills and abilities in radio-TV newswriting. At first, you might find that trying to write the way people talk is difficult, because most of the writing you've done in your life so far has been done in a more formal style for school assignments and perhaps for various print media. Don't get depressed and don't give up. Keep practicing. Keep writing. It may take some time for you to master the techniques of radio-TV newswriting, but with enough patience and practice, you'll be able to do it.

This workbook is divided into three main sections. In the first section, you'll be introduced to many of the theoretical, philosophical and practical aspects of radio-TV newswriting. We'll cover style, techniques, methods and mechanics. You'll get plenty of examples and models. In the second section, we'll cover some of the major legal and ethical concerns in radio-TV newswriting. In the third section, you'll get a chance to practice what you've learned. You'll be asked to write stories from wire copy, news releases, fact sheets and reporters' notes. You'll get a chance to write just about every type of radio-TV news story that an entry-level staff member in a radio or television news department would be expected to know how to write.

Unless your instructor tells you differently, when you do any of the assignments in this workbook, you have to imagine yourself working as a newswriter at KCTI-AM or KCTI-TV. Both stations are committed to airing quality newscasts. The stations are located in Midcity. Midcity could be just about anywhere, but think of it as a medium-sized city in the Midwestern portion of the United States. Listed below are some facts you need to know about Midcity.

● MIDCITY, USA

Population:	958,471
Top executive officer:	Mayor Ronald R. Moore

Legislative body:	Nine-member Board of Supervisors

Court system:

Municipal Courts: civil cases involving amounts of no more than $5,000 and all criminal cases where the possible term of incarceration is one year or less. These criminal cases are called misdemeanors, petty misdemeanors and violations.

Superior Courts: civil cases involving amounts of more than $5,000 and all criminal cases where the possible term of incarceration is more than one year. These criminal cases are called felonies.

Schools (public):

Midcity Unified School District. Grades kindergarten through high school. Enrollment: 78,110.

Higher education (public):

Midcity University. Offers B.A./B.S., M.A./M.S., Ed.D., Ph.D., J.D. and M.D. degrees. Enrollment: 20,000

Midcity Community College. Offers A.A./A.S. degrees. Serves people interested in vocational areas and those preparing to transfer to four-year colleges and universities. Enrollment: 10,000

Higher education (private):

West Midcity Community College. Offers A.A./A.S. degrees. Serves people interested in vocational and technical areas but offers transfer-oriented programs, too. Enrollment: 3,500

● RADIO-TV NEWS TERMINOLOGY

Before we get into the specifics of writing news for radio and television, you should be familiar with terms associated with radio-TV news.

Actuality: Taped comments from a news source. Used in radio. Also called *tape cut, cut* or *soundbite.*

Actuality Story: Radio news story that contains an actuality. Newscaster reads related copy prior to and after actuality is aired.

Air People: People who read news on the air. News announcers. Newscasters. On-air people. On-air personalities. Talent. Anchors.

Anchor: Person who reads news on air. See *Air People.*

A-roll: Term left over from days when film was used in TV news. Refers to audio portion of story—reporter narration, stand-ups and soundbites.

Assignment Editor: Person who decides which stories will be covered and which reporters will cover them.

Audio Tape: Magnetic tape used to record sound.

Backgrounding: Doing research on a source or topic/subject prior to conducting an interview or going into the field to gather information.

Backtiming: Exact timing of a newscast or newscast segment (story or stories plus credits and/or close) to ensure it is aired correctly. If the final segment is 1:00, a newscaster must begin the final segment with exactly 1:00 remaining in the newscast. Despite careful planning, newscasters quite often must either read extra stories or cut material in order to begin the final segment at the precise time.

Bite: Short for "soundbite." A source's comments on audio tape or videotape.

Breaker: Unexpected news event. Examples: fires, traffic accidents, plane crashes, hostage situations, murders.

Bridge: Transition between story elements, stories or newscast segments.

Briefs: Short news stories—usually about :10-:15 each.

B-roll: Term left over from days when film was used in TV news. Refers to action and activities captured on videotape.

Bulletin: A breaking news story of great importance that moves on a wire service. Also called a *flash* or an *urgent*. Can also refer to an interruption of regularly scheduled programming by a newscaster to provide information about a breaking news story.

Bump: Brief sentence or sentence fragment read by a newscaster or off-screen announcer about an upcoming story or segment. Usually aired before a commercial break. Object is to entice audience members to stay tuned. Titillating aspects of a story often played up. Also "bumper." Sometimes called a *tease, toss* or *promo*.

Cart: Short for "cartridge." Plastic shells that contain audio tape. Used in radio for actualities, voicers and wraparounds.

CG: Short for "character generator."

Character Generator: Computer used to superimpose letters, numbers and words on a television screen.

Chromakey: Electronic process used to insert graphics and other visual material behind a television newscaster. A computer graphic, picture, still frame, video or other visual material is electronically substituted for a color, usually blue or green, that is painted on the news set.

Chyron (chiron): Brand of character generator.

Close-up Shot: Video scene with a restricted field of view. Examples include a hand that fills the TV screen or a single face. Camera usually as close to action as possible.

Copy: News story written to be aired. Can also refer to material that is used to produce a news story (i.e., "source copy" or "wire copy").

Cover Shot: Video scene that covers a large or wide area. Usually shows much action, lots of people or a large expanse of territory. Also known as an *establishing shot, long shot* or *wide shot*. It establishes the visual parameters for a succeeding series of scenes. Camera usually 15-20 feet from action.

Credits: Superimposed list of names that is seen at the end of TV newscasts. Names include people responsible for putting the newscast on the air and station management personnel.

Cut: Short for "tape cut." An actuality or soundbite.

Dateline: Geographic location where a news story was written and/or placed on a wire service feed. Usually found at the beginning of wire service stories. See *Wire Copy*.

ENG: Short for "electronic news gathering." Refers to the use of portable videotape equipment, computers and other sophisticated technologies.

Evergreen: A story that can be aired just about any time. Little or no time-sensitive content. Usually a feature story.

Eyewash Video: Video scenes that are not directly related to what is being read by a newscaster. For example, in a story about test scores for high school students, video of students wandering around campus might be shown. Also called *wallpaper video*.

Feature: "Soft" or "light" news story. Examples: personality profiles, restaurant reviews, movie reviews, humorous pieces. Can be used to describe special newscast segments. Examples: "Keeping Fit," "Troubleshooter," and "Consumer Watch."

File: To present a report. Can be used to describe a place where information is stored—i.e., computer files, file folders.

Fill Copy: News stories that are not expected to be aired but could be used to complete a newscast that is running unexpectedly short.

Flash: See *Bulletin*.

Freeze Frame: A single frame or scene from a videotape that can be locked in and shown to viewers. Also called a *still frame* or *still store*.

Graphic(s): Visual material that appears on the television screen. Examples: pictures, slides, charts, supers, still frames and other electronically generated images.

Hard News: Reports of timely and significant events and issues.

In: Short for "incue."

Incue: First three or four words of an actuality, voicer or reporter package.

Intro: Introduction. Copy for newscaster to read to introduce actualities, soundbites, voicers or videotape stories.

Key: Short for "chromakey."

Kicker: Final story of a newscast—often humorous. Designed to leave audience members with a good, upbeat, positive feeling. Also called a *zipper*.

Lead: First sentence or two of a news story. Designed to grab audience interest and let them know what the story is going to be about.

Lead-in: Introduction to an actuality, soundbite, voicer or reporter package. See *Intro*.

Lineup: List of stories and other material in the order they are to be used in a newscast. Also called a *rundown*.

Live Shot: Airing news events, interviews or reporter stand-ups as they occur from a remote location away from the studio/station.

Matching Point: Scene in video that requires precise coordination with narration by a newscaster or reporter. Audience members MUST hear about what they're seeing at the precise time the scene appears. A matching point normally occurs when a major person, place or thing appears in video.

Medium Shot: Video scene that contains a somewhat limited amount of material. Usually restricted to fewer than three people. Camera approximately 8-12 feet from action.

Narration Track: Copy read onto tape by a reporter for a voicer, wraparound or package. Also called a *voice track*.

Nat Sound: Short for "natural sound."

Natural Sound: Actual noises recorded at the scene of a news event or news-gathering activity. Ambient sound.

News Release: Information sheet from a business, institution or agency. Usually has a public relations function. Also called a *press release*.

On-air People: See *Air People*.

Open: Standard beginning music and/or announcer portion of a newscast.

Out: Short for "outcue."

Outcue: Final three or four words of an actuality, voicer or reporter package.

Pad Copy: See *Fill Copy*.

Personality: See *Air People*.

Personality Feature: Story that focuses on an aspect of the life and times of one person. Sometimes called a *personality profile*.

Personality Profile: See *Personality Feature*.

Press Release: See *News Release*.

Producer: Person responsible for the content and organization of a newscast.

Promo: See *Bump*. Usually refers to copy that is read and/or video that is shown during or between non-news programming. Designed to entice audience members to watch an upcoming newscast.

Prompter Copy: Copy prepared for a teleprompter.

Pronouncer: A phoneticized guide to help a newscaster pronounce a word or name correctly.

Reader: News story that a newscaster reads without actualities, soundbites or videotape. May include the use of chromakey graphics.

Remote: A live shot or segment. Reporting crew files material from a "remote" location away from studio/station.

Reporter Bridge: Stand-up used as a transition between story aspects or locations.

Reporter Package: News story in which reporter narration is coupled with taped comments from news sources. Videotape used in packages for television news.

Rip-and-Read: Reading wire copy on air without rewriting it.

ROSR: Short for "radio on scene report." A live or taped report from the scene of a news event. Reporter describes what he or she sees, hears and/or does. Much like an eyewitness account.

Round Robin: A series of related news stories that air back-to-back. A newscaster introduces the first story, but until the entire segment is completed, reporters handle the transitions between stories without returning to the newscaster. Reporter A tosses to reporter B and so on.

Rundown: See *Lineup*.

Shot List: Chronological order of individual video scenes in the final edited version of a videotape story.

Silent-Sound: Television news story that combines an anchor voice over and a soundbite or full-volume natural sound. Also called a *VO/SOT* or *studio package*.

Slug: Abbreviated title or summary for a story. Usually one or two words. Often placed in upper left or right corner of news script. Example: Dog Bite

Soft News: Feature stories that usually are timeless. See *Feature*.

SOT: Short for "sound on tape." Sound recorded in sync with picture on videotape.

Soundbite: Videotaped comments from a news source. Usually, only the news source is seen in the videotape. Often used as a synonym for *actuality* in radio.

Soundpop: See *Soundbite*.

Source Copy: Material used as a basis for writing or rewriting a story for air. Examples: wire copy, newspapers, news releases and reporters' notes.

Stand-up: Story segment where reporter is seen speaking directly to camera.

Stand-up Close: Stand-up used to end a reporter package.

Stand-up Open: Stand-up used to begin a reporter package.

Still Frame: See *Freeze Frame*.

Still Store: See *Freeze Frame*. Also refers to the process of saving single frames/scenes of video or other graphics in a computer.

Studio Package: Story voiced by newscaster. Includes videotaped action and one or more soundbites. Also called a *VO/SOT*. Can also refer to bringing a reporter into the studio to do a story during a newscast.

Super(s): Letters, numbers and words superimposed on a television screen by a character generator.

Tag: Ending sentence or two that an anchor reads following an actuality, soundbite, voicer or reporter package.

Tag Line: Final sentence or two spoken by a reporter in a package or voicer. Used for identification purposes. Usually includes the geographic location of the events, the reporter's name and the call letters of the station. Example: "From North Midcity, I'm Terry Kegel for KCTI News."

Tail: See *Tag*.

Talent: See *Air People*.

Talking Head: See *Soundbite*. Usually only the head and the top of the shoulders of the news source are seen. Sometimes used as a synonym for a *TV reader*. Only the head and top of the shoulders of the newscaster are seen on screen.

Tape: Audio tape or videotape.

Tape Cut: An actuality or soundbite.

Tease: See *Bump*. Also "teaser."

Teaser Lead: Lead that "teases" audience members into paying attention because it leaves out important information that will be revealed later in a story. Also called a *suspended interest lead*.

Teleprompter: Device that allows television newscasters to read copy without having to look away from the studio camera lens. Mirrors or electronics used to reflect words over the front of the camera lens.

Toss: See *Bump*. Also refers to comments that one on-air personality makes to another right before the other personality begins speaking. A transition between anchors.

Track: Short for "narration track" or "voice track."

TRT: Short for "total running time." Refers to length of story from first word to last word, including all actualities, soundbites, voicers, packages.

Urgent: See *Bulletin*.

Video News Release: Complete video story, soundbites or B-roll sent to TV news departments by companies, organizations or agencies. Usually serves a public relations function. Also "VNR."

Videotape: Magnetic tape used to record sound and picture in sync.

Visual(s): See *Graphic(s)*. Material used to enhance a story. Examples: pictures, slides, supers, videotape or electronically generated graphics.

VNR: Short for "video news release."

VO: Short for "voice over."

Voice Over: Television story in which a newscaster reads copy while video is seen by the audience.

Voicer: Radio news story introduced by a newscaster but narrated by a reporter live or on tape.

Voice Track: See *Narration Track*.

VO/SOT: Short for "voice over/sound on tape." A voice over combined with a videotaped comment from a news source. See *Silent-Sound*.

Wallpaper Video: See *Eyewash Video*.

Wire Copy: News stories provided over computer networks by the Associated Press (AP), United Press International (UPI) and others.

Wrap: Short for "wraparound." Also "wrapper."

Wraparound: Radio reporter package that combines one or more actualities or soundbites sandwiched between segments of reporter narration. The reporter's voice is "wrapped around" the actualities.

Zipper: See *Kicker*.

Radio-TV
Newswriting

A Workbook

P A R T 1

Radio-TV Newswriting Philosophy, Style and Methods

● **REWRITING**

All news stories should be rewritten from source copy. They should not be simply retyped or rearranged versions of the source copy. You should write stories in your own words, trying to *tell* what you know to audience members. If you do a good job, the newscaster will be able to sound as if he or she is *telling* a story to friends rather than *reading* a story to strangers.

A good habit to get into to enhance the chances that you will really rewrite source copy rather than simply retype or rearrange source copy is to make physical or mental notes from the source copy and then put it aside. Use your notes, NOT the source copy, as the basis for your story. Since you won't have the source copy staring you in the face, you won't fall back on the same tired phrasing used in the source copy. You'll be much more likely to create a new, more understandable and listenable story.

Rewriting is important for a number of reasons. It should be done to help give your station a distinct sound from other stations in town. Most of the other stations will likely get the same source copy you receive. In order for your station to sound different from any other, you need to take the facts from the source copy and express them in an individualized manner.

Rewriting should lead to improved conversationality, too. With careful rewriting, the copy should become more conversational, clearer and more understandable. Add some sparkle and zest. Try to make your copy come alive. Paint vivid "word pictures" for audience members. Take them places they've never been before. Show them things they've never seen before.

Rewriting allows you to update and freshen source copy. Be a proactive newswriter. Do some news gathering. Make some phone calls. Ask around the newsroom. Check files and computer databases. Try to find out if situations have changed or if new information has been discovered and released. Don't be satisfied with simply passing along the same old, tired facts, figures and quotes. Search for fresh information. Journalism is supposed to be a never-ending search for truthful information. Newswriters should contribute to such efforts.

Rewriting forces you to evaluate the information in the story critically. If crucial or important information is missing, search for it and add it to your story. Don't be content to use the source copy as your only source of

3

information. Fill in the information gaps that occur regularly in source copy by checking with other people, organizations, agencies, departments and databases.

If something doesn't seem right to you in a story, check it out. Use your common sense and your critical-thinking skills. Look for errors. Don't pass along inaccurate or bogus information. Do whatever you must to confirm facts and figures that seem suspicious. Modify such things if your fact-checking turns up new, more accurate information. Always "DO THE MATH!" Check addition, subtraction, multiplication and division. Perform such procedures as a way to check the accuracy of data included in source copy. DON'T PASS ALONG INACCURATE OR MISLEADING INFORMATION! Be part of the solution to poor journalism; don't help perpetuate the problem.

Rewriting allows you to stress a new or different angle from what is stressed in the source copy. You might be able to concentrate on something buried in the story. You might be able to come up with a local angle for a state, national or international story. Whenever possible, look for ways to use the source copy as a starting point for gathering the information you need to write a good story. Too often the source copy is both the beginning and the end of information gathering. It shouldn't be. Put your own creative reporting skills into practice to develop the story into something more interesting and more significant.

Stop and Write

List five main reasons for rewriting source copy.

1.

2.

3.

4.

5.

• MAKE IT INTERESTING

As you look at the source copy, think about what audience members need to know and what they'll find interesting. Emphasize those aspects in your story. The traditional "who, what, where, when, why and how" of journalism is a good place to start. Be sure you include answers to the 5 W's and H in your story.

Traditional news values or news elements give some guidance as well. Look for significance—how important things are and how many people are affected. Look for prominence—who's involved and what expertise do they have and/or what positions do they hold in society. Look for proximity—how close to home did the events occur and/or were any local people involved. Look for timeliness—how recently did the events occur. And look for human interest aspects—oddity, conflict, emotional appeals, heroism, achievement, romance, sex, animals and humor.

Research into why people become news consumers provides some help, too. Uses and gratifications research has found that people read, listen to and watch news because they want to be informed and reassured about their community, state, nation and world. They want to know what's going on and they want to feel confident that they're making good decisions. They want information that will help them get the most out of life. They want "news you can use." Work hard to find out how events and issues will likely affect your audience members. Help them to gain a better understanding of the meaning of the significant events, issues and developments of the day.

Help people make sense of the various worlds in which they live. Strive to help them understand the attitudes and the behaviors of newsmakers. Help people gain insights into why newsmakers say what they say, believe what they believe, value what they value, support what they support, dream what they dream and do what they do.

Most people like to hear the opinions of others so they can test their own opinions. They like to be intellectually stimulated. They like to be challenged.

Most people like to hear and see exciting developments. They like to find out about the interesting things that interesting people do.

Most people like to be entertained, too. They like offbeat, humorous stories. They like to hear and see feature stories about people with unusual hobbies and jobs.

Some of the many other standard things that people seem interested in include costs, benefits, advantages, disadvantages, pros, cons, historical perspectives, likely future developments, alternatives to the status quo, winners, losers, causes, effects, size, frequency, number, steps, procedures, processes, demographics, requirements, limitations, parameters, theories and hypotheses. Try to include as many of such things as you can in your stories. You and your audience members will be glad you did.

Stop and Write

List five news values/elements that radio-TV newswriters should stress in their stories.

1.

2.

3.

4.

5.

● TAKE CONTROL

You should want to be in charge when you write radio-TV news copy. You should want to be responsible for deciding just how the information will be presented. Having a "can do, take charge, I'm in command" attitude will make you a better writer. You'll be more careful. You'll be more precise. You need to have an open mind, of course, but you also need to be decisive, assertive and bold.

A bit later in the workbook we'll be covering various acceptable techniques, styles, methods and options. Your job will be to select the best way to communicate from among such choices. Accept the challenge with gusto. Relish the power.

Never leave anything to the whim of the newscaster. Never let a newscaster decide how to pronounce an unusual word or name. Never let a newscaster decide how to interpret an abbreviation. Never let a newscaster decide how to read a string of numbers. You take control. You decide how such things should be read. By leaving nothing to chance, you'll become a better writer.

Stop and Write

Why is it so important for radio-TV newswriters to have a "take charge" attitude when they write their copy?

Let's move now to some specific tips for how to write quality radio-TV news copy.

● KEEP IT SIMPLE

Research has shown that audience members rarely give their undivided attention to radio-TV newscasts. Most of the time, people are reading, eating, driving or talking while newscasts are on. We'll be trying to capture their attention with our writing, of course, but, since audience members aren't hanging on every word a newscaster says, it is important to use simple, easy-to-understand words and sentence constructions.

Don't confuse or perplex audience members. Don't force them to translate or decipher complex words and sentence constructions. Confused and perplexed audience members often become angry audience members and angry audience members usually don't remain loyal listeners or viewers of your station.

Don't try to impress audience members with your extensive vocabulary. Your goal is to communicate important information to as many people as you can. Use one-syllable words rather than multi-syllable words. Use common, everyday words rather than pedantic, obscure words.

Example: Use *bruise* NOT *contusion*

Example: Use *cut* NOT *laceration*

Example: Use *rain, sleet* or *snow* NOT *precipitation*

Use simple declarative sentences as often as possible. The comfortable subject-verb-object order is a good one. Avoid cluttering up your sentences with a lot of phrases and clauses. Tell your story simply. Tell your story directly. Write the way you'd share what you know with a friend. Write the way you talk. Write so your copy sounds conversational.

Example (poor): Waiting until he was sure he had enough votes in the legislature to kill any attempts to override his approval of the measure, Governor Sorenson signed the state income tax cut bill late last night.

You wouldn't talk like this would you? Don't write radio-TV news copy like this then. Write it simply. Write it clearly. Write it directly.

Example (better): Governor Sorenson signed the state income tax cut bill late last night. He waited until the last minute to be sure he had enough votes in the legislature to squash any attempts to override his approval.

Another reason why it's important to write simply is because audience members don't get a written record of the information. They can't go back and reread or recheck something. They must get it right the first and only time they hear it from a newscaster. Make it as easy as possible for audience members to get the information they need.

Stop and Write

Why is it so important for radio-TV newswriters to keep their copy simple and clear? List and discuss three tips for how to achieve that goal.

1.

2.

3.

● TALK UP, NOT DOWN

Respect the intelligence of your audience members. Don't talk down to them in your copy. Writing simply does not mean writing simplistically. Give audience members the information they need and want in a clear, direct manner. You'll turn them off and they'll turn you off if you talk down to them. They have too many other ways to acquire the information they want. Most won't put up with being assaulted by copy that insults their intelligence.

Research has shown that most audience members have several distractions when they attempt to listen to radio news or watch TV news. Your job is to attract and hold their attention for as long as possible. You'll succeed more often if you envision your listeners and viewers as sophisticated news consumers rather than a bunch of semi-interested, semi-literate clods.

Why is it dangerous for radio-TV newswriters to underestimate the intelligence of audience members?

● RHYTHMIC WRITING

Your writing should have a rhythm. It should have a flow. When a newscaster reads it into a microphone, it should sound as if he or she is talking informally with friends. One way to improve the flow of your copy is to vary sentence length. On average, sentences should be no more than about 20 words. Vary the lengths, though. Perhaps a few sentences can run longer than 20 words and many sentences should run much shorter than 20 words. Again, the key is to try to capture the rhythmic patterns of everyday conversations.

Use transitions to improve the flow between different aspects in a story. Avoid awkward and abrupt changes in topics within stories. Look for linkages.

Example: *in addition, meanwhile, however, on the other hand, in other matters, also, too, but, and*

Be a ruthless editor of your own copy. Change what doesn't sound conversational. Rework sentences. Make some longer. Make some shorter. Never be satisfied.

Writing is a dynamic process. Rarely is your first attempt your best effort. Be your own worst critic. Rewrite and rewrite until you get it right.

Stop and Write

List three ways a radio-TV newswriter might improve the flow of his or her story.

1.

2.

3.

● SOUND MATTERS

How your copy *sounds* is critical. Since audience members won't be reading your prose, you must force yourself to "sound out" the copy as you write it. As you write, you constantly should ask yourself, "How does this sound?" Of course, after you finish a sentence, you should read it aloud to be sure it sounds conversational.

Don't content yourself with simply looking at the copy on paper or on a computer screen. Get into the habit of "sounding out" your sentences. If you have the time, record your copy and play it back. Be a tough judge. Does it sound conversational? Would you talk this way with friends? Will it sound as if the newscaster is *telling* a story and not *reading* a script?

Stop and Write

Why should radio-TV newswriters be concerned about the "sound" of their copy?

● WRITE TIGHTLY

Time is precious in radio-TV newswriting. You don't have much of it in which to tell your story and quite often you don't have much time to write your story, so be concise in your writing. Trim the fat of needless words. Get to the point, tell why it's important and move on. You want to be conversational, of course, but be a merciless editor of your own copy. Critically analyze every word to be sure it plays an essential role in conveying the information you feel is important.

Many adjectives and adverbs can be eliminated from your copy. *There is* and *there was* are good candidates for elimination, too. *That* can often be eliminated. Normally, *that* is useless when placed between a verb used to convey attribution and a paraphrased comment.

Example (poor): He says *that* the measure will bankrupt the state.

What's *that* doing in there? Get rid of it!

Example (better): He says the measure will bankrupt the state.

Don't go crazy with your elimination of all *that*s, though. Sometimes *that* is needed to improve the flow of a sentence or to clarify meaning.

Example: He feels that Simpson is innocent.

Example: He feels Simpson is innocent.

Which of the above examples sounds best to you? They both could probably be used, but *that* works in this example, don't you think?

Stop and Write

Why is it important to write "tight" radio-TV news copy?

● NAMES MAKE NEWS

Pronounce It Right

Just about every story you write will have at least one or two names in it. It's important that you spell every name correctly, of course, but it's also important to include a pronunciation guide for difficult to pronounce names. If a newscaster mispronounces a name, it hurts the station's credibility.

If you come to a name that you're not sure how to pronounce, there are several things you can do:

1. Check with other members of the news staff.
2. Check name pronunciation lists provided by the wire services.
3. Check with associates of the person.
4. Check with the person directly. You'll be surprised how appreciative and cooperative most people are when you make a special effort to be sure to pronounce their name correctly.

Once you know how to pronounce a name correctly, pass the information along to the appropriate newscaster AND place a phoneticized, syllablized version of the correct pronunciation directly above the correctly spelled version.

(MA-drihd)	(Muh-DRIHD)
Example: Jim Madrid	**Example**: Jane Madrid
(Keye-moo-KEE)	(Keye-MOO-kee)
Example: Alice Kaimuki	**Example**: Allan Kaimuki

Use upper-case letters for the emphasized syllables and place the pronunciation guide in parentheses. The United Press International Pronunciation Guide is included on the next page for your convenience. You don't always have to follow the guide exactly. The important thing is to be sure newscasters know how to pronounce unusual names. You can modify the UPI guidelines or develop your own guidelines to ensure proper pronunciation. As long as the newscaster knows the correct pronunciation, you've done your job.

United Press International Pronunciation Guide

Vowels

A	ay	for long A as in *mate*		**O**	oh	for long O as in *note* or *though*
	a	for short A as in *cat*			ah	for short O as in *hot*
	ai	for nasal A as in *air*			aw	for broad O as in *fought*
	ah	for short A as in *father*			oo	for O as in *fool* or *through*
	aw	for broad A as in *talk*			u	for O as in *foot*
					ow	for O as in *how* or *plough*
E	ee	for long E as in *meet*				
	eh	for short E as in *get*		**U**	ew	for long U as in *mule*
	uh	for hollow E as in *the*			oo	for long U as in *rule*
	ay	for French long E *with* accent as in *Pathé*			u	for middle U as in *put*
	ih	for E as in *pretty*			uh	for short U as in *shut*
	ew	for E as in *few*				
	e	for middle E as in *per*				
I	eye	for long I as in *time*				
	ee	for French long I as in *machine*				
	ih	for short I as in *pity*				

Consonants

k	for hard C as in *cat*		z	for hard S as in *disease*
s	for soft C as in *cease*		s	for soft S as in *sun*
sh	for soft CH as in *machine*		g	for hard G as in *gang*
ch	for hard CH or TCH as in *catch*		J	for soft G as in *general*

Weird Words

Include a pronunciation guide for unusual words, too! If you think a newscaster might have trouble with any word, you're better off including a phoneticized, syllablized version directly above the correctly spelled version.

Include a pronunciation guide every time the word is used if it is extremely difficult to pronounce; however, for most words, a pronunciation guide on the first reference is all you'll need to include. Be sure you tell the newscaster how to pronounce the word, too!

Stop and Write

Create a pronunciation guide for the following names and words. We'll assume you've checked with appropriate sources to develop your pronouncers.

1. Eric Timothy Wulfemeyer

2. Nevada

3. Jay Schroeder

4. facade

5. Reginald Smythe

6. La Jolla

7. Erika Donnerstein

8. fiduciary

9. Kirsten Kadooka

10. segue

First and Last Names

Use the full first and last name of a person on the first reference in a story. For each subsequent reference, use the last name only. This applies to both men and women. Occasionally on subsequent references, a person's title can be used instead of his or her last name, but generally it's best to use the last name.

Example: Midcity Mayor Ronald Moore has a big problem and he's not exactly sure what he's going to do about it. Moore wants to remodel his office, but the City Attorney won't let him.

Example: Midcity Mayor Ronald Moore has a big problem and he's not exactly sure what he's going to do about it. The mayor wants to remodel his office, but the City Attorney won't let him.

Unknown Names

Avoid using unknown names at the beginning of stories. Unknown names won't attract attention and audience members will likely miss the names before the subject matter grabs their attention. Instead of starting a story with an unknown name, try using a person's title or some other identifying characteristic—age, where he or she lives, a physical characteristic or what makes him or her newsworthy. Give the name in the second sentence. This technique is called "delayed identification."

Example (poor): Eric Wulff is the best POG player in the world. He proved it last night.

Example (better): A 25-year-old Midcity man is the best POG player in the world. Eric Wulff proved it last night.

Example (better): The best POG player in the world lives in Midcity. Eric Wulff earned his title last night.

Example (better): A six-foot-two, 225-pound Midcity man can flip little milk bottle caps better than anybody in the world. Eric Wulff proved it last night by winning the World POG Championship.

Middle Names and Initials

Usually, middle names or initials are NOT used in radio-TV newswriting; however, if a person's middle name or initial has become a recognized part of his or her celebrity or if a person requests that his or her middle name or initial be used, then include it.

Example: Edward R. Murrow

Example: T. S. Eliot

Example: George Washington Carver

Example: F. Scott Fitzgerald

Example: Hillary Rodham Clinton

Example: John F. Kennedy

Example: Mary Chapin Carpenter

Example: Billy Ray Jones

Identification

Quite often it is important to differentiate one "Jane Smith" or "John Smith" from all the other people with the same name in your community. It's especially important to make clear which Jane Smith is in the news when you're writing about a crime, accident or award. Not only do you want to avoid potential legal troubles, you want to be sure audience members understand who deserves the credit or blame for successes or failures.

There are three main ways to differentiate people:

1. You can give their titles or occupations.
2. You can give their addresses.
3. You can give their ages.

TITLES. The preferred way to identify a person is to include some title, job description or a description of what it is that has made a person newsworthy. Titles are generally included BEFORE a person's full first and last name.

Example: The Director of the Midcity Help Center, Gloria Perkins, says most people have some kind of emotional problem.

It's usually not a good idea to place an ordinary title after a person's name as is often done in newspapers. It's simply not conversational. Read the following example and see if you don't agree.

Example: Gloria Perkins, the director of the Midcity Help Center, says most people have some kind of emotional problem.

A modified "title-after-the-name" construction can be used, though. It sounds more conversational.

Example: Gloria Perkins, who is the director of the Midcity Help Center, says most people have some kind of emotional problem.

The key, of course, as always, is to write in a conversational manner. If you think placing a title after a person's name sounds better than placing it before his or her name, do it.

Another way to handle titles and names is to use "delayed identification." Use the title by itself in one sentence and the name in the next sentence.

Example: The Director of the Midcity Help Center says most people have some kind of emotional problem. Gloria Perkins says it's just a sign of the times.

When a title is extremely long, it can be quite a mouthful for a newscaster and quite an earful for audience members. You need to take steps to make such titles more palatable. Inordinately long titles can be placed after a person's name or they can be broken down into smaller bits and shared with audience members over several sentences.

Example (poor): The Chairman of Midcity Citizens Against Unlawful and Unnatural Uses of Public Open Space Land and Recreational Areas, Stan Davis, told the Board of Supervisors it should get tough with land developers.

Example (better): The chairman of a local pro-open-space group says the Board of Supervisors should get tough with land developers. Stan Davis is the head of Midcity Citizens Against Unlawful and Unnatural Uses of Public Open Space Land and Recreational Areas. He says the developers have had things their way for far too long.

Example (better): The chairman of a local pro-open-space group says the Board of Supervisors should get tough with land developers. Stan Davis, who is the head of Midcity Citizens Against Unlawful and Unnatural Uses of Public Open Space Land and Recreational Areas, says the developers have had things their way for far too long.

ADDRESSES. Another way to differentiate people is to list their address. A person's address is normally reported in one of the following ways:

Example: Susan Lynn, who lives on Mast Avenue, won the race.

Example: Susan Lynn, of Mast Avenue, won the race.

There is a hierarchy of address specificity. You could report the full street address, including street numbers and even apartment numbers. Such specificity is rarely needed, though. In fact, in most cases, you should strive to be as vague as you can be with someone's address and still differentiate him or her from all other people in the community with the same name. This lack of specificity protects people's privacy and informs audience members, but still protects the station from potential legal problems from people who have the same name as someone in the news.

Take a look at the following examples. They move from very specific to very unspecific. In your own writing, evaluate each case carefully and determine the appropriate degree of specificity needed. Crime, accident and award stories usually demand the greatest degree of specificity.

Example: Susan Lynn, of 7-6-9-1 Mast Avenue in East Midcity, won the race.

Example: Susan Lynn, of the 76-hundred block of Mast Avenue in East Midcity, won the race.

Example: Susan Lynn, of Mast Avenue in East Midcity, won the race.

Example: Susan Lynn, of East Midcity, won the race.

Example: Susan Lynn, of Midcity, won the race.

AGES. The third way to differentiate a person is by including his or her age. Ages are normally reported BEFORE a person's full first and last name, but there are at least three acceptable ways to report a person's age.

Example: The winner was 20-year-old Susan Lynn.

Example: The winner was Susan Lynn, who is 20-years-old.

Example: The winner was Susan Lynn. She is 20-years-old.

Usually, a person's age should only be reported when it is a pertinent part of the story. For example, if a person is unusually old or young to be involved in something, then his or her age should be mentioned. Age should be used as a differentiating device only if you cannot determine a person's title or address or if you want to be sure there will be no mistaking just who is involved in the events and issues at hand.

Remember, complete identification—title, address and age—is often used in crime, accident and award stories. Use your own judgment, though. Just be sure that audience members clearly will know which "John Smith" or "Jane Smith" newscasters are talking about.

SUBSEQUENT REFERENCES. Most of the time, identification is used only with the first reference to a person, along with a person's full first and last name. After that, only a person's last name is used. There are exceptions, of course. Sometimes writers use a person's title only or some other descriptive word or phrase without a name on a second or third reference.

Examples: the Mayor, the Senator, the President, the chef, the police officer, the child, the student, the man,

the woman

Occasionally, especially in feature stories or in stories that involve young children, first names can be used in place of last names on second and third references. Be careful, though. Fight the urge to become too cutesy or familiar when naming names.

Example: The suspect, 15-year-old Matthew Zavesky, says he's innocent. Matthew says he has an air-tight alibi

that proves he was nowhere near the statue when the toilet-paper hanging occurred.

Normally, it's not a good idea to use a person's age or title in place of his or her first name. You shouldn't use a person's age as a substitute for his or her last name, either. Again, there are exceptions, but it's best to include titles and ages with full first and last names.

    Example (poor): The 20-year-old Lynn won the race.

    Example (poor): The 20-year-old won the race.

    Example (poor): Postal worker Lynn won the race.

Stop and Write

Rewrite the following in correct KCTI news style.

1. Gerald P. Stagg, 57, 9843 Dove Ct., was charged with robbery.

2. Marilyn D. Vargas, 66, prof. of biology, Midcity University, died today.

3. John R. Means, 25, 4101 Hamilton Blvd., was injured in the crash. Mr. Means suffered contusions, lacerations and abrasions.

4. Edward F. Whittler, Dist. Atty. of Midcity, will run for re-election. The 45-year-old Whittler has held the job since 1984.

5. Susan L. Morton, 38, chairwoman, Midcity Board of Supervisors, will fly to Washington next week. Supervisor Morton will testify on Wednesday.

● ATTRIBUTION

    Attribution is the "who says so" in sentences. It is the source of your information. In radio-TV newswriting, attribution is normally included at the beginning of a sentence, because that's the way most people provide attribution in their everyday conversations. Placing attribution at the beginning of a sentence also allows audience members to know right away that newscasters are reporting the opinion of others and NOT giving their personal opinions.

Example: Mayor Ronald Moore says too many local businesses are mismanaged.

In radio-TV news, attribution is rarely reported in the middle of a sentence or at the end of a sentence as is often done in newspapers.

Example (poor): Too many local businesses, Mayor Ronald Moore says, are mismanaged.

Example (poor): Too many local businesses are mismanaged, Mayor Ronald Moore says.

Attribution is not necessary in every sentence, but it is MANDATORY when a statement is clearly opinion. Whenever a piece of information is a known and indisputable fact, you don't need attribution.

Stop and Write

Which of the following sentences need attribution and which do not?

	Needed	Not Needed
American cars aren't as good as Japanese cars.	[ ]	[ ]
Most college athletes are poor students.	[ ]	[ ]
The oil companies are ripping-off the public.	[ ]	[ ]
Fire destroyed the Desert Mirage Hotel in Las Vegas.	[ ]	[ ]
A jet crashed at the Midcity Municipal Airport.	[ ]	[ ]
Three men died in a traffic accident in East Midcity.	[ ]	[ ]
A short circuit caused the fire.	[ ]	[ ]
Governor Sorenson signed the bill.	[ ]	[ ]
The Padres won the game.	[ ]	[ ]
George Washington was the best President.	[ ]	[ ]

● ATTRIBUTION WORDS

Says and *said* are the most acceptable attribution verbs. Other acceptable, but less frequently used attribution verbs include *according to, adds, added, reports* and *reported*. Don't worry about coming up with a lot of synonyms for *says* or *said*. Most of them aren't conversational and many of them have a tinge of editorial comment associated with them.

Examples (poor): *claims, asserts, declares, vows, proclaims, exclaims, points out, discloses, warns, promises*

Of course, if a source really warns, promises or declares, you can report such revelations and use the appropriate attribution verb. Generally, though, sources simply say things, so you should simply say they say things.

Avoid using *states* or *stated*. They're too stiff and formal. How often have you used or heard someone use *states* or *stated* in everyday conversations? For that matter, how often do you use any other attribution verbs besides *says* or *said*?

Example: Melissa states we should go to the football game.

Example: Melissa asserts we should go to the football game.

Example: Melissa claims we should go to the football game.

Example: Melissa declares we should go to the football game.

Example: Melissa says we should go to the football game.

Which of the above examples sounds the most conversational to you? The last one, right? Use *says* and *said* as your attribution verbs.

Stop and Write

Rewrite the following in correct KCTI news style.

1. The program won't help the homeless, Mayor Ronald Moore stated.

2. "It's a scam," Supervisor Susan Morton claims, "because it just can't be done for that amount of money."

3. The bid by the Hayward Corporation isn't the lowest, Kettner proclaimed, but it's the best.

4. "Sen. Donald Smith should be impeached," Sen. Lydia Lowenstein announced.

5. Five people died in the fire, Midcity Fire Capt. Linda Smith pronounced.

• QUOTES

When you want to quote a source and you don't have an actuality or soundbite to use, it's usually best to paraphrase a source's words.

Example (original): "Midcity desperately needs an anti-litter campaign," Supervisor Emily Jebb said.

Example (rewrite): Supervisor Emily Jebb says Midcity needs an anti-litter program.

Direct quotes are difficult and awkward to handle in copy, but if you must quote a source exactly, be sure to let audience members know you're quoting the exact words of a source. Remember, audience members can't see quotation marks and you can't expect newscasters to indicate direct quotes by changing the inflection in their voices.

Example: Supervisor Emily Jebb said, and we're quoting her exactly. . .

Example: Supervisor Emily Jebb says, and we're quoting now . . .

Example: Supervisor Emily Jebb says, and these are her exact words . . .

Example: Supervisor Emily Jebb says, and this is the way she expressed it . . .

Avoid the old, "quote, unquote" method of indicating you're quoting the exact words of a source. It's too awkward and certainly not very conversational.

Example (poor): Supervisor Emily Jebb said, quote, Midcity desperately needs an anti-litter campaign, unquote.

Most of the time, paraphrasing is the best way to handle comments from sources, but you should quote exactly when a statement is extremely controversial, complex or unusually well-expressed. In most cases, paraphrasing allows you to condense a source's words and you can often make his or her points more understandable. Be careful not to change the meaning of what a source has said when you paraphrase. Improve the phrasing, but keep the meaning.

Stop and Write

Rewrite each of the following sentences twice. The first time keep the quote a direct quote. The second time paraphrase the quote.

1. "Mayor Ronald Moore is the worst mayor in the United States," Supervisor Roger Hedgeman claims.

    A. (Direct Quote):

B. (Paraphrase):

2. "Whittler's plan is the lamest, most inane thing I've ever heard," Mayor Moore barked.

   A. (Direct Quote):

   B. (Paraphrase):

___

● CONTRACTIONS

Use contractions! They're informal and conversational. Instead of *it is,* use *it's*. Instead of *cannot,* use *can't*. Instead of *does not,* use *doesn't*. Instead of *they are,* use *they're*.

Example: It's going to be a long week for the Midcity Mustangs. They can't seem to shake the injury jinx.

Sometimes, the formality or severity of a situation dictates a more formal writing style. In addition, occasionally you might want to be sure there will be no confusion about what is positive or negative, pro or con, a go or a no go. In such cases, DO NOT use contractions.

Example: Governor Sorenson says he will not sign the bill.

Example: Governor Sorenson did not sign the bill.

Example: Governor Sorenson says it is not the proper time.

● ADJECTIVES AND ADVERBS

Be careful when you use adjectives and adverbs. In fact, avoid them more often than not. Often they are opinion words or value judgment words that are best reserved for editorials. Let your verbs add color and action to your writing.

When you want to describe something, keep it simple and direct. If the mayor delivers a five-minute speech, then write he delivered a five-minute speech. Don't write that he flawlessly delivered a hard-hitting, cleverly worded speech. What's hard-hitting, flawless and cleverly worded to you, might be wishy-washy, flawed and sarcastic to audience members. Simply report what the mayor said and let the audience members decide what adjectives and adverbs to attach to the mayor's words.

● VERBS

Use present tense verbs as much as possible. They make newscasts sound current and add snap. Of course, if using a past tense verb makes more sense, then use it. You might try the present perfect tense of the verb, though. It makes a sentence sound more current than using the past tense.

Example (past tense): District Attorney Edward Whittler resigned today.

Example (present perfect tense): District Attorney Edward Whittler has resigned.

Example (present tense): District Attorney Edward Whittler is ready for a new challenge. He has resigned to

take a teaching job at U-C-L-A.

Use active voice verbs more often than passive voice verbs. The active voice improves the flow of a newscast and makes it sound more immediate. The passive voice slows the flow. The passive voice can be recognized by the presence of a past tense verb, present perfect tense verb or a past perfect tense verb preceded by a form of the verb *be*. Quite often, a prepositional phrase is included in the sentence as well.

Example (passive voice): Midcity University was awarded a 500-thousand-dollar grant by the Ford Foundation.

In the above example "was awarded" is the passive verb and "by the Ford Foundation" is the prepositional phrase. To change a passive voice verb to an active voice verb, take the object of the preposition, "the Ford Foundation," and make it the subject of the sentence.

Example (active voice): The Ford Foundation awarded a 500-thousand-dollar grant to Midcity University.

Creating a simple, active voice, declarative sentence normally is the best way to go; however, sometimes the passive voice works better. Use your judgment. If you want to emphasize a noun, then use it first in the sentence. Whenever you use a passive voice verb, though, at least try turning the sentence around to make it active and see if you don't feel it sounds better in the active voice.

Example (passive voice): The fire was caused by a short circuit.

Example (active voice): A short circuit caused the fire.

Example (passive voice): Two suspects have been arrested by police.

Example (active voice): Police have arrested two suspects.

Example (passive voice): The man was bitten by the dog.

Example (active voice): The dog bit the man.

Stop and Write

Change each of the following passive voice sentences to active voice sentences.

1. The fire was caused by faulty wiring.

2. The winning run was driven in by Tony Gwynn.

3. The plan was proposed by Prof. Laurie Leitner.

4. The getaway car was driven by Marvin P. Muller.

5. First place was awarded to Sheryl Tennessen by the judges.

● NUMBERS

Write numbers so newscasters can read them easily. You don't want newscasters to have to think about or decipher numbers as they read them. Stations use different styles for writing numbers, but one common method is to spell out all single-digit numbers, use numerals for all two- and three-digit numbers and then use a combination of the rules to deal with numbers that include four or more digits.

In other words, the numbers one through nine are written out as words. The numbers 10 through 999 are written using numerals. Numbers equal to or greater than one-thousand are written using a combination of the rules depending on how you want a number voiced. Always write out the words *hundred* (for numbers greater than 999), *thousand, million, billion* and *trillion*.

Example: 1,600 becomes one-thousand-600 or 16-hundred

Example: 15,011,035 becomes 15-million-11-thousand-35

Example: 487,332 becomes 487-thousand-332

Example: 23,157 becomes 23-thousand-157

Use hyphens to keep together number strings and make numbers look like a complete unit. Try to keep your use of numbers to a minimum, though. Numbers can give meaning to your stories, but audience members can be overwhelmed if you use too many numbers. Rarely should a single sentence contain more than two numbers.

Try to avoid beginning a sentence with a number. It looks odd and might confuse or startle a newscaster. In addition, audience members might miss it. If you must start a sentence with a number, consider spelling out the number even if it is larger than one digit.

Example (poor): 15 people died in the crash.

Example (better): Fifteen people died in the crash.

Example (better): The crashed claimed 15 lives.

Be careful about writing "a thousand" or "a million." If the newscaster pronounces the "a" with the hard "ay" instead of the soft "uh," audience members might hear "eight thousand" or "eight million." Either write "one-thousand" or "one-million" or include a pronunciation guide.

               (uh)
Example: Nearly a thousand people died in the quake.

Example (better): Nearly one-thousand people died in the quake.

Stop and Write

Write the following numbers in correct KCTI news style.

1. 7_____

2. 5-hundred _____

3. 1,064 _____

4. 76,897 _____

5. forty-nine_____

Approximations

Round off numbers whenever precise figures are not necessary. Think about what amount you want audience members to remember and provide a general, meaningful and memorable number that will help audience members get a sense of just how big something is. Be sure to include an "approximation" word BEFORE giving the rounded-off number to let audience members know you're not providing exact figures.

Example: 24,989 becomes "about 25-thousand"

Example: 2,991 becomes "almost three-thousand"

Example: 13,978 becomes "nearly 14-thousand"

Example: 994 becomes "slightly less than one-thousand"

Example: 38,042 becomes "slightly more than 38-thousand"

There are other approximation words, of course. The important thing is to be sure to use one of them when you round off numbers.

Stop and Write

Round off the following numbers. Use a different approximation word or phrase for each example. Use correct KCTI news style.

1. 49_____

2. 998_____

3. 1,503 _____

4. 5,008 _____

5. 749,996 _____

Translate Numbers

If you can replace a number with some reference that is more recognizable, understandable or meaningful to audience members, be sure to do it. Be careful about making obscure or "inside joke" references, though. Your job is to communicate information to audience members. If a number will do the best job of communicating, use the number. If a representative, familiar reference will do the best job of communicating a number, use it.

Example: 5,200 feet becomes "about a mile"

Example: 11 inches becomes "about a foot"

Example: 2,035 pounds becomes "slightly more than a ton"

Example: 126 ounces becomes "slightly less than a gallon"

Example: a rock with a 30-inch circumference becomes "a rock the size of a basketball"

Fractions and Decimals

Spell out fractions and decimals. Spell out "point," too. Use your judgment about whether it's best to use a fraction or a decimal. Try both out in the sentence and determine which one communicates best and fits best with the subject matter and flow of the story.

Example: 3/4 becomes "three-fourths"

Example: 3/4 becomes "75-percent"

Example: 1.25 million becomes "one-and-a-quarter-million"

Example: 1.25 million becomes "one-point-two-five-million"

Of course, you can always translate fractions and decimals into whole numbers.

Example: 3/4 or 75% becomes "three out of every four"

Example: 1.25 million becomes "one-million-250-thousand"

Ordinals

Use the same rules for ordinals that you use for numbers. Single-digit ordinals should be spelled out as words. Double- and triple-digit ordinals should be written as numerals with added appropriate letters to indicate the ordinal. Use *st, nd, rd* and *th*.

Example: first, second, third, fourth, fifth, sixth, seventh, eighth, ninth

Example: 21st, 32nd, 43rd, 54th, 161st, 272nd, 883rd, 999th

Days of the month and addresses often use ordinals.

Example: June 21st, July 22nd, August 23rd, September 24th

Example: 21st Street, 22nd Street, 23rd Street, 24th Street

Lists and the order of finish in some sort of competition often use ordinals.

Example: Midcity is the ninth largest city in the United States.

Example: Murphy finished 26th.

Example: Most people thought the eighth grade was the best.

Example: Miss Midcity was the first runnerup.

Stop and Write

Rewrite the following in correct KCTI news style.

1. 2-feet-11-inches _____

2. 50% _____

3. 9.75 million _____

4. 8th place _____

5. October 31 _____

Time Elements

WHEN events occur is often very important. Be reasonably specific with your use of time, though. Don't simply use *today* for every story. Most of what is reported on radio-TV newscasts happened today. *Today* is too general and it becomes tedious when it's used in every story. Be more specific. Use *this morning, this afternoon, this evening, minutes ago* and other more definite references.

Example: early this morning, late this afternoon, right before we came on the air, moments ago, mid-morning,

sunrise, sunset, noon, midnight

When you include very specific time-of-day references, do it using numerals to express both the hour and the minutes. Use a colon to separate the hour from the minutes. If there are no minutes, use two zeros.

Example: 12:00, 1:15, 2:30, 3:45, 4:10, 5:25, 6:50, 7:05, 8:35, 9:52, 10:20, 11:59

Example: His plane arrived at 11:30 this morning.

Example: The performance will begin at 8:00 this evening.

Example: The rally will be held at 2:15 tomorrow afternoon.

(oh-five)
Example: Set your V-C-R for 9:05 tonight.

Note the last example above. It's a deviation from the normal method of reporting individually voiced numbers, but 9:0-5 looks too odd, don't you think? Occasionally, you'll run into situations that demand a little flexibility and creativity. You might even have to modify a rule or two. Again, your job is to help a newscaster communicate information easily and effectively. Do what it takes to get the job done.

Rarely use *A.M.* or *P.M.* when you report time. Most people don't use such references in their everyday conversations, so you shouldn't use them in your radio-TV newswriting. Substitute *this morning, this afternoon* or *this evening* for *A.M.* and *P.M.*

Example: 10:00 a.m. becomes "10:00 this morning"

Example: 2:30 p.m. becomes "2:30 this afternoon"

Example: 6:45 p.m. becomes "6:45 this evening"

If you want to include the word *o'clock* as part of a time reference, just add it after the numerals. Normally, *o'clock* is used only with on-the-hour references. It sounds odd when you report minutes, too.

Example (poor): 10:15 o'clock this morning

Example (poor): 2:30 o'clock this afternoon

Example (poor): 6:45 o'clock this evening

Example (better): 10:00 o'clock this morning

Example (better): 2:00 o'clock this afternoon

Example (better): 6:00 o'clock this evening

When you report hours and minutes that are not associated with time of day, use the standard rules for writing numbers. Spell out the appropriate time designations, of course.

Example: Jones finished in two-hours-10-minutes-and-24-seconds.

Example: The winning couple danced for a grand total of 49-hours-two-minutes-and-17-seconds.

Stop and Write

Rewrite the following in correct KCTI news style.

1. 12:00 p.m. _____

2. seven o'clock _____

3. 7-30 a.m. _____

4. 10:45 p.m. o'clock _____

5. 8-hours-twenty-minutes-16-seconds _____

Number Exceptions

There are a few exceptions to the standard rules for numbers, as you've probably seen in some of the examples. Time of day, sports scores, vote totals, addresses and phone numbers should be written with numbers even if they are single digits. Linking up the number strings with hyphens (or a colon) is critical, though. It helps eliminate the odd-looking single digit.

    Example: The phone number is 2-9-2-2-8-9-5.

    Example: He gave his address as 1-9-8-3 Ronson Road.

    Example: The tipoff is set for 5:15 tonight.

    Example: The Padres beat the Dodgers 5-to-4.

    Example: The vote was 296-to-139.

• SYMBOLS

Never use such symbols as $, %, &, ¢. Always spell out symbols as words. Make it easy on newscasters.

    Example: dollars, percent, and, cents

Link up the words you substitute for symbols with the appropriate numbers.

    Example: $50 million becomes "50-million-dollars"

    Example: 50% becomes "50-percent"

    Example: 50¢ becomes "50-cents"

    Example: Ben & Jerry's becomes "Ben-and-Jerry's"

Stop and Write

Rewrite the following in correct KCTI news style.

1. $20 _____

2. 8% _____

3. 5981 45th St. _____

4. The Dodgers won five-four. _____

5. 75¢ _____

• ABBREVIATIONS

Few abbreviations are used in radio-TV newswriting. Newscasters could have trouble reading them correctly and audience members might not recognize them or be familiar with what they stand for. In most cases, simply spell out abbreviated words and the names of organizations, especially on the first reference. Subsequent references often can be made using an abbreviation, though.

Example: The National Organization for Women, which is known as NOW, will hold its annual convention in Midcity next year. NOW chapters from every state will be represented.

Example: The National Collegiate Athletic Association has a new president. And William Richardson plans some major changes for the N-C-A-A.

Never abbreviate the names of states or countries, days of the week, months, titles, ranks, address designations or "junior" or "senior" when used as part of a person's name.

Example (poor): Calif., CA, Mon., Dec., Sgt., Rd., Ave., St., Jr., Sr.

Example (better): California, Monday, December, Sergeant, Road, Avenue, Street, Junior, Senior

It is permissible to use "Mr." or "Mrs." in copy. Such courtesy titles are rarely used in radio-TV newswriting, but they can be used to differentiate one spouse from the other in a story.

Example: Steven and Sally Jones were both injured. Mr. Jones suffered a broken leg and Mrs. Jones suffered cuts and bruises.

Some organizations have become so well known by their abbreviated titles that if you used the full name, audience members might not recognize it. Use your judgment. Communicate. If you have any doubts at all that audience members might not recognize an abbreviated title, spell it out on the first reference and then use the abbreviated title for subsequent references.

Example: F-B-I or Federal Bureau of Investigation?

Example: C-I-A or Central Intelligence Agency?

Example: Y-M-C-A or Young Men's Christian Association?

Sometimes you want the abbreviated title to be read as a word and not as a string of letters. If so, don't place hyphens between letters and include a pronunciation guide above the capitalized abbreviation.

    (NA-suh)
Example: NASA

    (Now)
Example: NOW

● INDIVIDUALLY VOICED ELEMENTS

I said earlier that everything in your copy should be written EXACTLY the way you want a newscaster to read it. You decide if you want letters or numbers announced individually or as part of a group or string. If you want a letter or number individually voiced, separate it from related letters, numbers or words by using a hyphen. Be sure to use capital letters.

Example: U-N, U-S, F-B-I, G-O-P, N-double-A-C-P, C-P-A, U-S-C

Example: The number to call is 3-9-5-8-1-8-2.

Example: The number to call is 3-9-5-81-82.

Example: He used to live at 1-0-2-6 Hill Street.

Example: He used to live at 10-26 Hill Street.

The number "0" provides an interesting dilemma sometimes. Should it be read as a number, i.e., "ZERO," or as a letter, i.e., "oh"? Again, you make the call. If you want a newscaster to say "zero," place the word *zero* in parentheses above the number "0." If you want a newscaster to say "oh," place the *oh* in parentheses above the number "0."

(zero)
Example: He used to live at 1-0-2-6 Hill Street.

(oh)
Example: He used to live at 1-0-2-6 Hill Street.

Stop and Write

Rewrite the following in correct KCTI news style.

1. NCAA_____

2. (619) 594-5450 _____

3. 26013 River Rd._____

4. Ph.D. degree _____

5. Team USA _____

● GRAMMAR, SPELLING AND PUNCTUATION

Follow the general rules of English grammar, spelling, punctuation and capitalization. Generally, it's best for a newscaster to see things in copy that he or she is used to seeing in other written materials. You don't want to present a newscaster with something that looks odd, different, unusual, misused or out of place. It could distract or confuse the newscaster and lead to mistakes

For example, if a word is normally capitalized in print media writing, capitalize it in your radio-TV newswriting. If you'd use a comma in your print media writing, use a comma in your radio-TV newswriting.

Some radio-TV newswriters use an ellipsis (three periods) in place of a comma. Such usage makes pauses more noticeable. If you choose to substitute an ellipsis for a comma, be sure to still use a single period to indicate the end of a sentence.

Example: The reasons for the cancellation were lack of time . . . lack of money . . . and lack of interest.

It's always critical to spell words correctly, of course. Remember, never replace the correctly spelled version of a word with a phoneticized version. Include the phoneticized pronunciation guide in parentheses above the correctly spelled version.

If you need to refresh yourself a bit on English grammar, spelling, punctuation and other language skills, consult one of the following books.

R. Thomas Berner, *Language Skills for Journalists*
Brian S. Brooks and James L. Pinson, *Working with Words*
E. L. Callihan, *Grammar for Journalists*
Lauren Kessler and Duncan McDonald, *When Words Collide*
Scott Rice, *Right Words, Right Places*
William Strunk, Jr. and E. B. White, *The Elements of Style*

● EDITING

Most of your editing of copy will be done on a computer; however, occasionally you'll need to make some minor changes on an already printed script. Keep your hard-copy editing of stories to a minimum, though. Remember, you're trying to help newscasters read the copy easily, so you can't use most of the standard print-media copyediting symbols. They aren't much help to a newscaster who's trying to read copy in a well-paced, authoritative manner. There is no place in radio-TV news for messy, marked-up copy. Generally, if you make a mistake, black out the mistake and print in the correct version above or next to the mistake.

Example: The murder weepon has not been found.

Very few of the standard print media copyediting symbols are used in radio-TV newswriting. The acceptable symbols include the following:

It's okay to use a word separation symbol (乚).   It's okay to use a "linking up" symbol (⌒).

It's okay to use a word(s) insertion symbol (Y).

Example: Lori Lynn will be in charge of the new unit.

Example: Lori Lynn will be in charge but not of the new unit.

Example: Lori Lynn will be in charge of the new unit.

Avoid using print-media copyediting symbols that would force a newscaster to do some on-the-fly translation to make sense out of the changes.

Do NOT use a letter or word transpositional symbol ($\mathcal{N}$) ($\sqcap\!\!\!\sqcup$).

Do NOT use a letter elimination symbol ($\mathcal{f}$).

Do NOT use a letter(s) insertion symbol ($\forall$).

Example (Do NOT use): The braodcast ran long.

Example (Do NOT use): Simpson said he was guilty not.

Example (Do NOT use): The introoduction took 20-minutes.

Example (Do NOT use): The trble has just begun.

Most stations allow no more than TWO editing marks or corrections per line of copy and no more than SIX editing marks or corrections per story.

Stop and Write

Correct the following using correct KCTI copyediting symbols.

1. The vote wll will be a close one.

2. The race is tooclose too call.

3. The election clearly will go down to the wire.

4. The vote surprised msot experts.

5. The victory was unexpted.

● COPY PREPARATION

1. Use standard-size sheets of paper.
2. Print on only one side of the paper.
3. Double-space copy.
4. Use upper-case and lower-case letters for newscaster copy.
5. For radio copy, use a 60-character line. (:03 per line)
6. For TV copy, use a 40-character line. (:02 per line)
7. Indent five spaces from the left margin for each new paragraph.
8. Use separate sheets of paper for each story.
9. NEVER divide words, numbers or hyphenated phrases at the end of a line and continue them on the next line.
10. NEVER break a sentence at the end of a page and continue it on the next page. Always end a page on a complete sentence.
11. Slug each story in the upper left corner with a one-word or two-word summary of what the story is about. Under the slug, list your name and the date.

Example: Jefferson Murder
             Wulfemeyer
             10/31/95

12. Place the TRT (Total Running Time) in the upper right corner.

Example: Jefferson Murder   TRT :30
             Wulfemeyer
             10/31/95

● LEADS

The lead for a radio-TV news story is like the headline for a newspaper story. It should grab interest. It should give audience members an idea of what the story is going to be about. It should set the tone for the story. It should NOT be written in newspaper headlines, though. It should be written in a clear, concise conversational manner.

Example (poor): Midcity man drowns in bathtub.

Example (better): A Midcity man drowned in his bathtub this morning.

Emphasis Lead

For most stories, you'll use an emphasis lead. It consists of the most important piece of information. It should be whatever you'd tell a friend if you bumped into him or her on the street.

Example: Hi, Lisa! Guess what I just heard? Mayor Moore has resigned.

Mayor Moore's resignation is the most important piece of information. Leading with it emphasizes its significance. Most of the time you'll want to get the "who, what, where, when and how" of each story in the first couple of sentences. The "why" of the story is usually saved for later, because more time is needed to explain it fully. Be sure to include the "why," though. It's critical.

Example: Three Midcity women died in a plane crash this morning.

Example: The prime interest rate is up again.

Example: Midcity University has a new football coach.

Example: The rain continues to fall in Southern California.

Example: Two men robbed a downtown Midcity bank this afternoon.

Blanket Lead

The blanket lead is more general than the emphasis lead. It covers a number of separate but related pieces of information or stories.

Example: The U-S Supreme Court ruled on four major cases today.

After you've let audience members know you're going to be talking about four separate cases, you can begin giving the details of each one. Use the blanket lead sparingly, though. Be sure all of the pieces of information or stories are truly related. Be sure they all belong in the same bed and under the same blanket lead.

Example: Governor Sorenson outlined his new five-point plan to pump some life into the state's sagging economy. (*Note:* After the lead, give the details of each point.)

Example: Six people died in traffic accidents over the weekend on Midcity streets. (*Note:* After the lead, give the details of each accident.)

Example: The Board of Supervisors has passed three new money-saving measures. (*Note:* After the lead, give the details of each measure.)

Example: Lots of gang-related trouble in Midcity overnight. (*Note:* After the lead, give the details of each troubling episode.)

Narrative Lead

The narrative lead starts with the first thing that happened and then you proceed through the story reporting the events in the order they occurred. It's truly like telling a story. The narrative lead usually is reserved for light, feature stories rather than more serious news events.

Example: A local construction worker was tearing up some floorboards in an old house on the east side of town this afternoon when he saw something shining out of a crack in the foundation. Miguel Ramos picked up the object, brushed it off and saw that is was an 18-90 50-dollar gold piece. He called us and asked if we'd find out how much it was worth. Well, we checked and it's valued at 175-thousand-dollars. Ramos plans to take the next couple of days off to celebrate his discovery.

Notice how the name of the worker is delayed until the second sentence. His title (or job description) is used in the first sentence. The "delayed identification" works well in this case.

Question Lead

Use question leads sparingly, if at all. A question lead sounds too much like a commercial.

Example: Are you sick and tired of feeling sick and tired?

A question lead runs the risk of getting an answer you don't want.

Example: Have you every thought about going back to college?

If audience members say "no," they're likely to tune out the story or worse, turn to a different station. A question lead often is difficult to read well and most of them aren't very conversational.

Example: A movie studio in Midcity?

Would you walk up to a friend and start a conversation like that? If not, don't write that way. Quite often, question leads are quickly followed by answers.

Example: Does Midcity Telephone really need a rate increase? Supervisor Roger Hedgeman doesn't think so.

Why waste the time asking a question if you're just going to give the answer in the next sentence? Get to the answer. That's why audience members have tuned you in.
Take a look at the following rewrites of the question leads used as examples in this section. Decide which seem better, the question leads or the rewrites.

Example: If you're sick and tired of feeling sick and tired, a Midcity doctor thinks she can help you.

Example: Going back to college can be a bit frightening for people over 40.

Example: Midcity could be the next Hollywood.

Example: Supervisor Roger Hedgeman doesn't think Midcity Telephone needs a rate increase.

Verbless Lead

Sometimes you can omit the verb in a lead. Instead of starting with "There was" or "There is," just tell what happened or is likely to happen.

Example: Another traffic-related death in Midcity last night.

Example: Lots of excitement at the Board of Supervisors meeting.

Example: Two more hats in the political ring for mayor this evening.

Example: Another big drug bust in East Midcity this morning.

Example: More rain in the forecast for tomorrow.

Vague or Teaser Lead

A lead is supposed to grab interest, but avoid trying to grab interest by being vague. Many radio-TV newswriters think they'll increase audience attention and interest by a vague reference to a person, event or issue. Their hope is that audience members will want to find out more about the odd and often confusing reference. This technique can backfire, though. Confused audience members might just turn to another station and some audience members might confuse the new vague lead with the preceding story.

Example: It wasn't his idea, but he's going along with it.

What if the above lead follows a story about the governor's analysis of a new tax-cut measure. Might not the audience become confused? Is the newscaster talking about the tax-cut story or a new story? Is the governor going along with the plan or not? Why create the possible confusion?

In addition, would you start a conversation with a friend using a vague-lead opening?

Example: Hi, Karen. It wasn't his idea, but he's going along with it.

Poor Karen. She'll probably wonder what the heck you're talking about. Whose idea? What idea? Who's he? And why are you starting a conversation in such an odd manner?

If you wouldn't talk this way to a friend, you should not be writing this way in radio-TV news. Be clear and direct in your writing.

Stop and Write

List and define six different types of radio-TV news story leads.

1.

2.

3.

4.

5.

6.

● BODY

Once you've written the lead, the rest of the story usually flows in a natural and logical manner. One way to organize a story is to think of it as a series of main points and supporting evidence.

You identify the main points of each story and then list the supporting evidence for each of the points. Supporting evidence would include such things as quotes, comparisons and statistics.

After writing your lead, list the appropriate supporting evidence for your main point. After you've provided enough supporting evidence for your first main point, move on to your second main point and provide the supporting evidence for it. Cover as many main points and include as much supporting evidence as you can in the assigned length for your story.

Example: Three Midcity Police officers pleaded innocent in Superior Court this morning to charges of racketeering and assaulting a federal agent. (*Main Point* 1)

John Wood, Lester Fulton and Marvin Katz face 14 counts of racketeering and assault. The charges were filed in connection with a meeting the officers had two months ago with a federal agent who was posing as a pawnshop owner. (*Supporting Evidence* 1)

The officers were charged after a month-long investigation turned up evidence of bribes and payments associated with an alleged "protection for hire" scheme. (*Main Point* 2)

The investigation involved F-B-I agents, Midcity Police and U-S Customs agents. (*Supporting Evidence* 2)

Stop and Write

Discuss an effective way to build the body of a radio-TV news story.

- ## ENDINGS

Ending a story can be almost as difficult as starting one. Most of the time, though, you simply finish with the last bit of supporting evidence for your final main point.

A great many stories can be concluded by providing a piece of "background" information about someone or something in the story. Examples include past accomplishments, related actions or activities and historical significance.

Example: Wulf's first book came out in 1985.

Example: Wulf is also the president of the Midcity Art Club.

Example: Only five other tenured professors have been dismissed in Midcity University's 75-year history.

You can end a story with information about what is going to happen or what is likely to happen in the future. Examples include the next step in a process and speculation on the chances of success or failure.

Example: Wulf's proposal will be voted on by the Board of Supervisors at next week's meeting.

Example: Wulf will be arraigned tomorrow.

Example: The bill now goes to the governor.

Example: The Senate is expected to vote on the measure sometime next week.

You can end a story by telling audience members how to obtain more information about the major people, events and issues covered in your story. Examples include names, addresses and phone numbers for people, departments, agencies and organizations.

Example: You can get more information about the program by calling the Midcity University College of

Continuing Education.

Example: If you want more information, call 2-8-3-55-45.

Example: Call us here at the station, if you need more information about the fun run.

Finally, you can end a story by making a clear connection to something mentioned at the beginning of the story. This "circle" technique or "tying the story up" is used quite often in feature stories.

Example: A Midcity artist has perfected an ice-carving method that makes it possible to do much more detailed

and intricate work than ever before.

Krystal Wulf uses lasers and micro-surgery tools to create ice miniatures. Her work is in such great demand

that she's had to quit answering her phone, because she's booked for the next six months.

Wulf says she's definitely carved out too much work for herself.

Stop and Write

List and define four different methods for ending a radio-TV news story.

1.

2.

3.

4.

● INTRODUCTIONS

Actualities and Soundbites

Introductions to radio actualities and videotaped soundbites serve two main purposes. The first, of course, is to grab the attention of audience members. The second is to prepare the audience for the information contained in the actuality or soundbite.

Use complete sentences for introductions. By using complete sentences, you maintain a conversational flow for the newscast. You also help lessen the impact of possible technical difficulties.

Example (poor): Mayor Moore is against the program, because . . .

(TAPE)

IN: "We'd get cheated on . . ."

OUT: ". . . a lot cheaper elsewhere."

TIME: :20

If the actuality doesn't play, the newscaster can't recover as well as if you'd used a complete sentence introduction.

Example (better): Mayor Moore is against the program, because he thinks it costs too much.

(TAPE)

IN: "We'd get cheated on . . ."

OUT: ". . . a lot cheaper elsewhere."

TIME: :20

If a technical difficulty occurs and the tape does not air, the complete sentence introduction allows a newscaster to either ad-lib or simply continue with the rest of the scripted copy more easily than the incomplete sentence introduction does. A pause is natural after a sentence, so after realizing that the tape is not going to play, the newscaster can continue without necessarily having to explain why the actuality failed to materialize. With an incomplete sentence introduction, the newscaster will be obligated to explain that a technical difficulty has occurred.

Avoid the "when asked if" method of introducing an actuality or soundbite. It has become a cliché in radio-TV news.

Example (poor): When asked if he thought the program was worth the money, Mayor Moore had this to say.

(TAPE)

IN: "We'd get cheated on . . ."

OUT: ". . . a lot cheaper elsewhere."

TIME: :20

Another construction to avoid is the "echo chamber." It occurs when the first words of the actuality or soundbite are exactly the same or very similar to the last words of the newscaster's introduction.

Example (poor): Governor Sorenson says it's time the state income tax was reduced to a reasonable level.

(TAPE)

IN: "It's time the state income tax was reduced to a reasonable level."

OUT: ". . . for all of us."

TIME: :15

Instead of creating the "echo chamber," try to encourage audience members to listen to the actuality or soundbite.

Example (better): Governor Sorenson says taxpayers deserve a break.

(TAPE)

IN: "It's time the state income tax was reduced to a reasonable level."

OUT: ". . . for all of us."

TIME: :15

Stop and Write

List and discuss three tips for writing effective introductions to radio actualities of television soundbites.

1.

2.

3.

Voicers and Packages

Whenever possible, try to incorporate some aspect of the story in the introduction to a reporter voicer or package.

Example: Lots of excitement at the Board of Education meeting this afternoon. And K-C-T-I reporter Jane

Baxter was there for all of it.

Example: More than five-thousand science fiction fanatics are in town for the annual convention of Science

Fiction Anonymous. K-C-T-I's Mark Zane sat in on the opening session.

Don't stretch too far to incorporate an aspect of the story in your introduction, though. If it doesn't flow well, don't force it. Be careful about using a pun or a "play on words." What you might think is clever and witty, audience members might find confusing or inappropriate. They might not understand the reference. They might not "get the joke." In addition, remember that audience members aren't going to see your words, so making clever use of homonyms will not have the desired effect.

Example: Midcity University started spring football practice today. We sent reporter Jeff Rodgers to **tackle** the story. (OUCH!)

Example: A new bed and breakfast inn opens this weekend in downtown Midcity. Reporter Diane Firestone went **"inn"** search of what it has to offer. (So?)

Example: A local turkey rancher is doing a booming business this summer. K-C-T-I reporter Carol Burns **gobbled up** the story. (YUCK!)

Example: The fish are really biting at Midcity-area lakes. Reporter Ed Murphy **baited his hook** to get a **line** on the story. (OH, NO!)

Example: A local lumber yard has come up with a plan to recycle wood chips. K-C-T-I's Tom Johnson **logs** in with this story. (PLEASE!)

Example: The new Midcity College of Optometry opens next week. Reporter Alicia McKay checked out the **"sight"** of the new campus. (YIKES!)

Example: The Midcity Community College women's basketball team is ranked number two in the country. Reporter Stephanie Davis went **one-on-one** to find out why. (HUH?)

If you can't logically and easily incorporate some aspect of the story in the introduction, simply use one of the traditional voicer or package introductions rather than stretch and create an inappropriate, goofy or nonsensical sentence.

Example: Jane Baxter reports.

Example: Mark Zane has the details.

Example: Alicia McKay has the story.

Example: Tom Johnson explains.

Example: Carol Burns has more.

Example: Ed Murphy has more on the story.

Stop and Write

Write five different reporter package introduction sentences for a story about twin koala bears being born at the Midcity Zoo. It's the first set of twin animals ever born at the zoo. The reporter is Grace Garcia.

1.

2.

3.

4.

5.

• WRITING FOR VIDEO

Writing for video requires much talent, training and practice. Not only do you have to write in a conversational, interesting and entertaining manner, you also have to be sure that the words and pictures complement each other.

Methods

Three basic methods are used to help ensure that words and pictures match.

1. Video scenes are edited together and then the words are written to match the lengths of the individual scenes.
2. The story is written first. Main people and things are identified and the time they are mentioned is noted. When the videotape editor puts together the video, scenes are cut to match designated cues for people and things.
3. The writer and videotape editor work together to decide how best to merge the words and pictures. Compromises are made along the way to be sure the best video is used and the most important information is included.

Of course, whenever possible, it's best to coordinate the writing of the script and the editing of the videotape into one, continuous process. Too often, though, there is not enough time to do this.

When you are asked to write a script for scenes that have already been edited, first take a long look at the "shot list" so you'll have an idea of how to organize your script. Study the order of the scenes. Determine when the major newsworthy people, places and things appear in the video and how many seconds you have between each major "matching point." Now try an "outline" of your story in the correct order. How much time do you have before the first matching point? The second? The third? How long to you have to talk about each major matching point? You want to be sure your words will closely match what audience members will see. The effectiveness of video stories depends, in part, on how well the words and pictures go together.

Guidelines

Some "writing for video guidelines" are included below.

1. Copy should flow in a natural, conversational, interesting and entertaining manner.
2. Follow all of the general rules for effective radio-TV newswriting.
3. Words and pictures should NOT conflict. What audience members see is what they should hear about. Strive for an "eye-and-ear marriage." Strive for a marriage of the visual and aural senses.
4. Avoid the "See Spot run. See Jane run. See Dick run." style of writing. You don't have to do "play-by-play" for most video scenes. You don't have to describe or identify everything that appears on screen. Audience members can see for themselves. Videotape will often tell its own story. Few or no descriptive words will be needed. Instead, use the time to EXPLAIN what audience members are seeing. Explain the significance. Explain the connections. Explain the meanings. Explain the ramifications. Explain the implications.
5. Be sure to identify each newsworthy person, place or thing the first time they appear on screen. You owe it to audience members to identify the major newsmakers, geographical locations and objects. The audio and video matching for such people, places and things should be perfect.
6. If the videotape has been previously edited, be sure to "underwrite" slightly. Have at least three seconds more videotape than you have narration. The extra tape is a mini-insurance policy just in case a newscaster takes longer to read a script than was anticipated. It also will give the director some flexibility in how he or she gets back to the newscasters in the studio after the narration ends.

Matching

Example: Shot List
1. Cover shot—Building and flames	:04
2. Medium shot—Smith	:04
3. Close-up shot—Trash can	:04
4. Medium shot—Firefighters	:04
5. Medium shot—Clean-up activities	:06

TAKE VIDEO/VO

The fire caused about 185-thousand-dollars damage to the old, wood and stucco building.

Fire Captain Linda Smith says the fire started when a smouldering cigarette ignited some old newspapers that were stacked in a trash can in an alley behind the Market Street store.

Firefighters battled the blaze for more than three hours before they brought it under control.

Clean-up operations will continue for several hours.

Notice how well the words match the pictures. Each full line of copy takes about two seconds to read. For a four-second scene, a newscaster should have two lines to read.

Example: Shot List

1. Cover shot—Valdez and project	:04
2. Close-up shot—Chart	:04
3. Medium shot—Wong and project	:06
4. Close-up shot—Snail in enclosure	:07

TAKE VIDEO/VO   The first prize went to Mark Valdez of Santana High School. His senior science project dealt with alternative energy sources and how they can be used in Midcity and neighboring cities.

Jennifer Wong of Woodrow Wilson High School took second place. Her project featured a study of the reproductive cycle of the common, everyday garden snail. She compared the cycle of the garden snail to that of freshwater snails.

Again, notice how the words match the video. When a new person or project is seen, it's talked about. Strive for this perfect match between audio and video. It will take practice, but if you have a good sense of the order of the scenes and their lengths, you'll soon master the art of the "eye-and-ear marriage."

Pauses

You can use pauses to help you achieve more specific matching. Don't overuse pauses, but whenever you have interesting and/or dramatic video, don't feel compelled to fill up every available second with newscaster narration. If the pictures can tell their own story, let them. This technique is especially effective if good natural sound accompanies the video.

You can indicate pauses by a series of periods or by typing in the word "PAUSE" in parentheses. Quite often the length of the pause is included as well.

Example: ....(PAUSE)...........................

Example: ....(PAUSE :04).........................

Example: Shot List
      1. Cover shot—Flood waters   :06
      2. Medium shot—People in boats   :04
      3. Close-up shot—Cow on roof   :06
      4. Medium shot—People filling sand bags   :09

TAKE VIDEO/VO   Floods continue to hammer the Midwest.

                         ....(PAUSE :04)......................

                         The water has risen as much as seven feet in

                         some areas...

                         Livestock have been especially hard hit.

                         ....(PAUSE :04)......................

                         Sand bags are reportedly in short supply as

                         people scramble to hold back the waters.

                         ....

More information on script formats and script timing is included at the end of this section.

Stop and Write

List and discuss five tips for effective television newswriting.

1.

2.

3.

4.

5.

● NEWSCAST ORGANIZATION

Putting together a newscast is difficult. It takes imagination and creativity to pull together into a coherent newscast all the wire-service copy, actualities, news releases, rewrites and reporter packages.

It helps if you have an organizational plan or model. If radio-TV newscasts are thrown together haphazardly without any real order or plan, the result is a jumble of unrelated stories that usually has little meaning to audience members.

Formats

The continuity and flow of a newscast can be improved greatly by using a definite organizational model. You might use one of the traditional newscast formats, or you might want to incorporate elements of several of the formats to develop your own. The important thing is to have a definite plan for organizing the newscast.

Four of the most commonly used formats are (1) significance, (2) subject/topic, (3) geographical, and (4) chronological.

In the *Significance Format,* stories are arranged in the order of their importance to and impact on audience members. The story that affects the audience the most is aired first, followed by the second most important and so on.

In the *Subject/Topic Format,* stories are grouped together according to subject or topic. For example, all police-related stories would be linked together, then all fire-related stories, education-related stories, government-related stories and so on.

In the *Geographical Format,* all local stories might run first, followed by state stories, regional stories, national stories and international stories.

In the *Chronological Format,* stories are arranged in the order they occurred. Usually, the most recent story is aired first, followed by the next most recent and so on.

Of course, elements of the various formats can be blended and you can have much overlapping of formats. For example, you might want to use the Geographical Format, but modify it slightly by using the Significance Format to order stories within each geographical area.

Strive for some logical newscast organization, though. Audience members will appreciate it and it will make your job as a producer much easier. If you have a model, you'll be able to arrange stories more quickly and have more time to deal with any last minute problems that arise.

Example: (The following stories are available for a newscast.)

1. Local traffic accident last night at 11:00 p.m. Two deaths.

2. Local house fire today at 2:00 p.m. Three deaths, $150,000 damage.

3. Los Angeles warehouse fire today at 9:00 a.m. Six deaths, $1.5 million damage.

4. Local gasoline prices to go up 10% next week. Hike announced at 3:00 p.m.

5. Midcity mayor appoints new member of Board of Supervisors at 11:00 a.m. Appointment ends two-month search.

6. Strike at local defense plant. Started at 8:00 a.m. 2,500 workers affected.

7. President appoints new Secretary of State at 10:00 a.m. Appointment is a surprise to journalists. It ends a month-long search.

8. Strike by New York City garbage workers moves into second week. Story moves on wire at 7:00 a.m.

The stories might be organized differently depending on which newscast format or model you decide to use.

SIGNIFICANCE
1. New Secretary of State
2. Gasoline prices
3. Local strike
4. New supervisor
5. Local fire
6. Traffic accident
7. New York City strike
8. Los Angeles fire

SUBJECT/TOPIC
1. New Secretary of State
2. New supervisor
3. Local strike
4. New York City strike
5. Local fire
6. Los Angeles fire
7. Traffic accident
8. Gasoline prices

GEOGRAPHICAL
1. Gasoline prices
2. Local strike
3. New supervisor
4. Local fire
5. Traffic accident
6. New Secretary of State
7. New York City strike
8. Los Angeles fire

CHRONOLOGICAL
1. Gasoline prices
2. Local fire
3. New supervisor
4. New Secretary of State
5. Los Angeles fire
6. Local strike
7. New York City strike
8. Traffic accident

Transitions

Transitions between stories act as the strings that tie a newscast together. They should flow naturally. They should not be contrived. Avoid the "and speaking of" or "in other news" transitions. They are overused and provide no real link from one story to another.

Look for natural connections, natural links. If they're not present, do without a transition. You don't have to have a transition between all stories. Just write them where they're appropriate.

Example: (Possible transitions between the Secretary of State story and the new supervisor story.)
1. Here in Midcity, the search is over this evening for a new member for the Board of Supervisors.
2. Midcity has a new government official, too.
3. The new Secretary of State wasn't the only new government official appointed today.

Example: (Possible transitions between the local strike story and the New York City strike story.)
1. Well, at least the strike at the defense plant isn't piling up garbage like a strike in New York City.
2. We've got our strike problems here in Midcity, but in New York City, a strike is really starting to stink.
3. The strike at the defense plant doesn't smell half as bad as a strike in New York City.

Example: (Possible transitions between the local fire story and the Los Angeles fire story.)

1. A fire in Los Angeles claimed twice as many lives and caused 10 times the damage as the one in Midcity.

2. More fire-related deaths in Los Angeles this morning.

3. Los Angeles was hit hard by fire, too, this morning.

Bumps, Tosses, Teases, Headlines and Promos

Newscasters often are asked to encourage audience members to stay tuned for news. Such pleas come during commercial breaks within non-news programming, just before newscasts begin, shortly after the beginning of newscasts and right before commercial breaks during newscasts. Bumps, tosses, teases, headlines and promos have become important weapons in the war to attract and hold an audience.

These interest-arousers are very brief. They usually concentrate on the most significant, interesting, weird or titillating aspect associated with an event or issue. Quite often they are written in newspaper "headlinese." They also can be phrased as questions.

Don't sensationalize teases, tosses, bumps, promos and headlines. Make them interesting, but don't exaggerate or embellish the facts and don't mislead audience members. You can be colorful. You can be mysterious. You can tempt. You can tantalize. You can pique the curiosity of audience members. Just be sure you're not overstating things and be sure you can deliver on the promises that you make with your teases, tosses, bumps, promos and headlines.

Example: What's happening to local gas prices? Stay tuned and we'll tell you.

Example: Gas prices are going up. Stay tuned.

Example: We'll all be paying more at the pump next week.

Example: It's really going to cost you at the gas station next week.

Example: A surprising new Secretary of State.

Example: The President pulled a fast one today.

Example: It's taken months, but we've got a new member on the Board of Supervisors.

Example: The hunt for a new Midcity Supervisor is over.

Example: Finally, the Board of Supervisors is at full strength.

Example: New York City really stinks tonight.

Example: The Big Apple is rotten.

Example: Another strike in Midcity.

Example: Another blow to the local economy.

Example: A fatal fire in Midcity this afternoon.

Example: Killer fires at home and in Los Angeles today.

Example: Our top stories tonight: New leaders at home and in Washington. Fatal fires. Gas prices on the rise and unhappy union workers. Stay with us.

Example: Marty has the story about a fire here at home. Marty?

Stop and Write

List and discuss five tips for effective radio-TV newscast organization.

1.

2.

3.

4.

5.

● SCRIPT FORMATS

It's important to become familiar with a variety of script formats. Some of the more common ones are included in this section. Remember, for KCTI scripts, use a 60-character line for radio (each line is :03 long) and a 40-character line for television (each line is :02 long).

Radio Reader

food stamps   TRT :20
wulfemeyer
5/21/95

      A new food stamp law takes effect next month. It's

designed to make it harder to cheat the system, but local

welfare officials say it's so confusing, they're not exactly

sure how to enforce the new regulations.

      The director of the Midcity Welfare Department, Karen

Murphy, has asked Washington to help her decipher the new

law. She expects an answer by the end of the week.

Radio Actuality

food stamps   TRT :30
wulfemeyer
5/21/95

A new food stamp law takes effect next month. It's
designed to make it harder to cheat the system, but local
welfare officials says it's so confusing, they're not
exactly sure how to enforce the new regulations.

The Director of the Midcity Welfare Department, Karen
Murphy, has asked Washington to help her decipher the new
law.

(TAPE)

IN: "We've asked the Department . . ."

OUT: ". . . clear up the mess."

TIME: :10

Murphy expects an answer by the end of the week.

Radio Voicer

food stamps   TRT :40
wulfemeyer
5/21/95

A new food stamp law takes effect next month. It's designed to make it harder to cheat the system, but local welfare officials say it's so confusing, they're not exactly sure how to enforce the new regulations.

K-C-T-I's Lori McFadden reports on what's being done to help sort things out.

(TAPE)

IN: "The Director of the . . ."

OUT: ". . . McFadden for KCTI News."

TIME: :22

Murphy expects to hear from Washington by the end of the week.

Radio Wraparound

food stamps   TRT :50
wulfemeyer
5/21/95

A new food stamp law takes effect next month. It's designed to make it harder to cheat the system, but local welfare officials say it's so confusing, they're not exactly sure how to enforce the new regulations.

K-C-T-I's Lori McFadden reports on what's being done to help sort things out.

(TAPE)

IN: "The Director of the . . ."

OUT: ". . . McFadden for KCTI News."

TIME: :32

NARRATION: The Director of the Midcity Welfare Department, Karen Murphy, thinks the new regulations stink. She says they're vague, contradictory and they have so many bureaucratic aspects that she's put in a call to Washington to help her sort things out.

MURPHY ACTUALITY :10

Murphy hopes the bureaucrats in Washington will revise the regulations to make them easier to enforce.
 Lori McFadden for KCTI News.

Murphy expects to hear from Washington by the end of the week.

TV Reader

food stamps
wulfemeyer
5/21/94

TRT :20

TALENT: A new food stamp law takes effect next month. It's designed to make it harder to cheat the system, but local welfare officials say it's so confusing, they're not exactly sure how to enforce the new regulations.

The Director of the Midcity Welfare Department, Karen Murphy, has asked Washington to help decipher the new law. She expects an answer by the end of the week.

TV Graphic

food stamps   TRT :20
wulfemeyer
5/21/95

TALENT: A new food stamp law takes effect

                                 next month. It's designed to make it

                                 harder to cheat the system, but local

                                 welfare officials say it's so confusing,

                                 they're not exactly sure how to enforce

                                 the new regulations.

TAKE MURPHY PIC   The Director of the Midcity Welfare

                                 Department, Karen Murphy, has asked

                                 Washington to help her decipher the new

                                 law.

TALENT: She expects an answer by the end of

                                 the week.

TV Voice Over

food stamps wulfemeyer 5/21/95	TRT :20
TALENT:	A new food stamp law takes effect next month.
TAKE VIDEO VO/SOT	It's designed to make it harder to cheat the system, but local welfare officials say it's so confusing, they're not exactly sure how to enforce the new regulations. The Director of the Midcity Welfare Department, Karen Murphy, has asked Washington to help her decipher the new law.
TALENT:	She expects an answer by the end of the week.

TV Soundbite

food stamps   TRT :30
wulfemeyer
65/21/95

TALENT: A new food stamp law takes effect

next month. It's designed to make it

harder to cheat the system, but local

welfare officials say it's so confusing,

they're not exactly sure how to enforce

the new regulations.

The Director of the Midcity Welfare

Department, Karen Murphy, has asked

Washington to help her decipher the new

law.

TAKE VIDEO/SOT FULL   IN: "We've asked the Department . . ."
OUT: ". . . clear up the mess."
TIME: :10

TALENT: Murphy expects an answer by the end

of the week.

TV VO/SOT

food stamps   TRT :38
wulfemeyer
5/21/95

TALENT:	A new food stamp law takes effect next month.

TAKE VIDEO VO/SOT	It's designed to make it harder to cheat the system, but local welfare officials say it's so confusing, they're not sure how to enforce the new regulations.
	The Director of the Midcity Welfare Department, Karen Murphy, has asked Washington to help her decipher the new law.

SOT UP FULL	IN: "We've asked the Department . . ."
	OUT: ". . . clear up the mess."
	TIME: :10

VO/SOT	Murphy expects an answer by the end of the week.

TALENT:	Local welfare officials estimate at least six-thousand people in Midcity will have their benefits reduced under the new law.

TV Reporter Package

food stamps   TRT 1:00
wulfemeyer
5/21/95

TALENT: A new food stamp law takes effect

next month. It's designed to make it

harder to cheat the system, but K-C-T-I

reporter Lori McFadden has found out

that the new regulations are causing

some problems for local welfare

officials.

TAKE VIDEO/SOT FULL   IN: "The new law has . . ."

OUT: ". . . McFadden for KCTI News."

TIME: :40

TALENT: Local welfare officials estimate at

least six-thousand people in Midcity

will have their benefits reduced under

the new law.

• REVIEW

1. Rewrite all source copy in your own words.

2. Write the way you talk. Use a conversational writing style.

3. Use simple, declarative sentences (subject—verb—object).

4. Keep your sentences short—about 20 words.

5. Write concisely.

6. Stress the impact of issues and events on audience members and provide the reasons behind the actions.

7. Include pronunciation guides for unusual words and names.

8. Place titles before names.

9. Place attribution at the beginning of sentences.

10. Use contractions.

11. Limit your use of adjectives and adverbs.

12. Use present tense or present perfect tense for most verbs.

13. Use active voice verbs as much as possible.

14. Spell out single-digit numbers as words. Use numerals for double- and triple-digit numbers. Use a combination of the rules for four-digit and larger numbers. Spell out as words *thousand, million, billion* in place of zeros.

15. Spell out symbols.

16. Spell out abbreviations.

17. Use the standard rules of English grammar, spelling, punctuation and capitalization.

18. Select the proper lead—emphasis, blanket, narrative, verbless.

19. Structure your story as a series of main points and supporting evidence.

20. Give your stories definite endings.

21. Use complete sentence introductions for actualities, soundbites, voicers and reporter packages.

22. Match the words and pictures in TV news stories. Avoid conflicts between what audience members hear and see.

23. Use a plan/model to improve newscast organization.

24. Use transitions between stories to help improve the flow of newscasts.

25. Use legitimate teases, tosses, bumps and headlines to help attract and hold the attention of audience members.

PART 2

Legal and Ethical Concerns in Radio-TV Newswriting

There are a number of legal and ethical concerns that confront radio-TV newswriters on a regular basis. Among the most common are libel, invasion of privacy, copyright infringement and sensationalism.

● LIBEL

Libel deals with defamation. *Defamation* is defined as the damage that can be done to a person's reputation or image when false communication about that person is made public. Any false communication that causes a person to be hated, ridiculed or shunned could be libelous. Any false communication that lowers a person in the eyes of his peers or that inhibits his ability to make money could be libelous. Under the law, libel is considered written defamation, but in most states, defamation that occurs on a radio or TV station is also considered libel.

Elements

One key aspect of libel, of course, is the truth and accuracy of information. Great care should be taken to ensure that information included in radio-TV news stories is as accurate and as truthful as possible. Stories should not be aired if there is some doubt concerning the veracity and validity of the information contained in them. If you must, hold stories until you can confirm or invalidate information. In addition, choose your words carefully. In the eyes of the law, people aren't murders, robbers, burglars, rapists, molesters or drug dealers unless they've been convicted in a court of law. Even then, many stations prefer to call them convicted murders, convicted robbers, convicted burglars, convicted rapists, convicted molesters or convicted drug dealers. People are occasionally convicted of crimes they did not commit.

Along the same lines, be careful about writing that people are HIV-positive, AIDS victims, gang members, adulterers, mentally ill, frauds, liars or cheats. Be sure you have your facts straight before you do any sort of name-calling or before you apply any sort of labels to people.

Simply quoting a source's comments does not protect the radio-TV newswriter from libel lawsuits. You and your station are responsible for almost everything that is heard or seen on your station. Just because you quote a source or a document, you're not absolved of that responsibility. There are some exceptions, but the best attitude to have is to be sure that everything aired is accurate and true.

There are a number of things that a radio-TV newswriter should know to reduce the chances of libel-related problems. For the most part, only living people can be libeled. The reputations of dead people are not as protected as those of living people. There are no absolutes in libel, though. Some recent cases have opened up the possibility that relatives of dead people and/or living people might have the right to sue to collect damages for the pain and emotional distress they suffer when their loved ones are defamed.

Generally, large groups of people cannot be libeled. The definition of "large" varies, but most courts seem to use figures between 25 and 50 as the upper limit. Writers should be careful with their words at all times, of course, but when writing about individuals or small groups of people, take special care. With groups larger than 50—Republicans, Democrats, teachers, professors, members of Congress—you have a bit more protection. Be extra careful when you describe groups, though. Using adjectives, adverbs, phrases and clauses tends to narrow the scope of your comments and it has the potential to create subgroups that might be small enough to sue you.

I once served as an expert witness in a libel case involving police officers from a small town. The reporter quoted a news source who said police officers in a city, especially those from this particular town, were "on the take." Had the reporter or his editor removed the qualifying clause (especially in ————-), it is unlikely that any police officers would have been able to win a libel suit. There were too many of them. But, by narrowing the focus to the smaller number (less than 10), the reporter and editor left their news organization open to a costly lawsuit. Choose your words with care. It can cost you and your news organization if you don't.

"Alleged"

Some radio-TV newswriters believe that using the word *alleged* as an adjective provides protection from libel suits. It doesn't. Most courts ignore *alleged* when it is used as an adjective and judge the case on what is left.

Example: alleged murderer BECOMES murderer

Example: alleged rapist BECOMES rapist

Don't bother using *alleged* as an adjective, but it can be somewhat useful as a verb. Courts seem more willing to accept *alleged* as a verb. Be sure a suspect has been charged with an offense before using *alleged* as a verb, though. To be perfectly safe, use *charged* as the verb.

Example: Police allege that Smith is the murderer.

Example: It is alleged by police that Smith is the rapist.

Example: Smith has been charged with murder.

Example: Police have charged Smith with rape.

Be sure a suspect has been charged with an offense before using either *alleged* or *charged*. If a person has not been formally charged with anything by law enforcement officials, withhold the person's name or be sure you call him or her a *suspect*. Many stations make it a policy not to name suspects until they have been charged, but you have a legal right to reveal the names of suspects. Just be sure you don't *charge* or *convict* them before authorities do.

Offenses

Knowing what a person must prove to win a libel case and what defenses can be used to win a libel case is critical.

When a person feels he or she has been libeled, he or she must prove four major things:

1. *Publication.* The defamatory material must have been made public. If it's on a radio or TV station, it's certainly "published."

2. *Identification.* The person must be identified in some way. Usually names are used, but pictures, descriptions, voices, videotape, an artist's rendering or other recognizable nicknames, caricatures and silhouettes can qualify.

3. *Defamation.* The person must be harmed in some way. Quite often this is done through demonstrations of lost income or potential income, but it can also mean emotional distress or damage to a person's reputation.

4. *Negligence.* The defamatory material must be shown to be false.

For public officials and figures, one additional element is added to the mix. Most elected and appointed government officials, movie stars, TV stars, radio personalities, authors, professional musicians and professional athletes must prove the airing of defamatory material was done with malice. *Malice* has been defined as knowing that what is being aired is false, but airing it anyway or having a reckless disregard for the truth by not checking the validity of information thoroughly enough before airing the defamatory material.

Defenses

Being familiar with the major defenses in a libel lawsuit should help radio-TV newswriters avoid potential problems. The defenses include:

1. *Truth.* Prove the veracity of the material included in the story. Truth is the best defense, but it is often illusive. Nevertheless, radio-TV newswriters should do everything in their power to be sure that what they include in stories is TRUE.

2. *Privilege.* Fair and accurate reports about what is said and done during official proceedings are protected. Generally, radio-TV newswriters can report on the testimony and actions during official trials, meetings and hearings without having to worry about being sued even if what is said and done might harm someone's reputation. The content of official documents—reports, files, minutes—is also protected. One caution: testimony, comments, actions or written materials that occur or are obtained outside of the "official proceeding or document" do NOT receive the same blanket protection.

3. *Fair Comment and Criticism.* When material or performances are offered to the public for approval or disapproval, radio-TV newswriters get some leeway to comment fairly and accurately on the quality of the offerings. Whenever a book, movie, TV program, radio program, song, album, concert, painting, performance, athletic feat or any other creative effort is offered to the public, radio-TV newswriters can evaluate the quality of the effort, production or performance. Again, the protection covers only what was offered to the public. Speculation on why a performance was so bad or good likely would not be protected.

Stop and Write

List and discuss five tips for avoiding potential libel suits.

1.

2.

3.

4.

5.

● INVASION OF PRIVACY

Invasion of privacy is both a legal issue and an ethical issue. We'll examine the legal aspects first. The ethical considerations will come later.

Categories

In the legal arena, invasion of privacy breaks down into four major categories:

1. *Invasion of Physical Solitude.* A person's physical privacy can be invaded by using hidden microphones or cameras to capture him or her saying and/or doing things on private property. Going onto private property without permission can lead to trouble, too.

2. *Private, Embarrassing Personal Facts.* Dredging up embarrassing personal facts about a person, even if true, can sometimes lead to trouble. "Truth with good motives" is one way to think about this area. Unless you have a good reason for dredging up some dirt on a person, even if the dirt is true, you run the risk of losing an invasion of privacy lawsuit.

3. *Misappropriation.* Using someone's name or likeness to endorse or sell something without permission can cause problems. It's best to be sure that a person really does support a cause or candidate before accepting someone else's claim to such support.

4. *False Light.* Putting someone in a false light in the public's eye can cause trouble, too. Careful matching of audio and video will help eliminate misidentifications and incorrect linkages. Avoid fabrication, exaggeration and embellishment. Don't make things up. Don't invent quotes and statistics. If you can't find out the information you need or you can't get the confirmation you need, hold the story or write the story using the information you have been able to confirm. Stick to the facts—the *justifiable* facts.

Defenses

The best defense in invasion of privacy lawsuits is "newsworthiness." It is defined as "what the public is interested in." Since the public is interested in just about everything, it's often hard for someone to win an invasion of privacy suit against the news media. Don't get over confident, though. Take care with material that may fall within any of the four categories of invasion of privacy. Be precise. Be detail-oriented. Be thorough. Be fair. Be skeptical. Be compassionate.

Another defense in invasion of privacy lawsuits is "consent." *Consent* is defined as getting a person's permission to do something or use some information prior to airing it. If you're concerned about a potential invasion of privacy, check with sources in the newsroom. Consent may have been obtained. Be sure the permission is written or at least recorded on tape.

Ethical Concerns

The ethical side of invasion of privacy grows out of the broad protection that journalists get when it comes to writing about the private lives of people, especially famous people. Legally, journalists can get away with quite a bit of prying into the private moments, joys, heartaches, triumphs, failures, strengths, weaknesses, glories and tragedies of people. Just because it's *legal* to do such things, doesn't mean it's *ethical* to do such things. Give some thought to what audience members *need* to know, not necessarily what they may *want* to know.

Be careful about giving out specific addresses of people. Do audience members really need to know exactly where newsmakers live? Be careful about naming people involved in accidents. Most stations take great pains to be sure family members of an accident victim have been notified before using the victim's name on the air. Be careful about delving into all the gory details surrounding crimes and accidents. Give some thought to the feelings of the relatives and friends of the victims. Again, how much do audience members really need to know? Take the ethical high ground. Don't pander to the baser interests and morbid curiosity that some people have when it comes to sex, crime and violence.

Perhaps invoking the "Golden Rule" might often be appropriate. Put yourself in the place of the people you're writing about. If you wouldn't want some information known if you were involved in a newsworthy incident, at least think about why you're about to include it in your story.

Stop and Write

List and discuss five tips for avoiding potential invasion of privacy lawsuits.

1.

2.

3.

4.

5.

COPYRIGHT INFRINGEMENT

Copyright protects the rights of authors, artists and other creative people to profit from their creations. Radio-TV newswriters must be careful not to pass off the work of others as their own. Not only is such plagiarism unethical, it can be illegal.

Concerns

Copyright concerns include the following:

1. Facts CANNOT be copyrighted. Only the way facts are presented—the style, the form and the art of the writing—can be copyrighted.
2. Copyright lasts the length of the author's life plus 50 years.
3. Most newspapers are NOT copyrighted every day.
4. Copyrights are obtained from the U.S. government.

Fair Use

Radio-TV newswriters get some leeway to use copyrighted material. Under what is called the "Doctrine of Fair Use," writers are permitted to include reasonably small portions of such material in news stories, reviews, commentaries and analyses.

Radio-TV newswriters need to be aware of some of the factors included in the determination of what is fair use:

1. *Purpose*. How and why was the material used? News gets a break.

2. *Amount*. How much was borrowed? Too much and even news people can get in trouble.

3. *Market Impact*. How did the borrowing affect the market for the original? Even a little borrowing might affect the profit margin of the original. Don't give away the ending to a book or movie.

4. *Public Interest*. Is the event or issue being reported significant enough to justify liberal borrowing from copyrighted material? The public's right and need to know must be great.

Bottom line on copyright? Do your own work. Rewrite source copy in your own words and you shouldn't have too much to worry about.

Stop and Write

List and discuss five tips for avoiding potential copyright infringement lawsuits.

1.

2.

3.

4.

5.

• ETHICS

Ethical issues abound in radio-TV news reporting, writing, editing and presentation. We won't touch on all of the concerns, but we will concentrate on some of the issues that most directly affect radio-TV newswriters.

Sensationalism

Sensationalism is a critical ethical issue. Radio-TV newswriters often find themselves under pressure to make something more out of a story than perhaps is warranted by the documented facts. Such pressure can come from a real or perceived need to boost ratings, hold on to a job, enhance career opportunities or get a raise.

There is no excuse, however, for embellishing or exaggerating facts and figures to heighten the drama or titillation of a story. Gory or emotional details should not be milked. Sex, crime and violence should not be played up. Play it straight. Let the facts speak for themselves. Share the natural drama and excitement of events and issues with audience members. Don't try to create an artificial aura of heightened drama and excitement. Audience members will see through such attempts eventually and they'll backfire on you. Over time, such attempts will actually drive audience members away from your station rather than attract and keep them as loyal followers of your station.

Fairness/Balance

It's important to be fair and balanced in your presentation of information. If you are including accusations and allegations about a person in a story, be sure to make every effort to get reactions and defenses from that person or his or her representatives.

You don't necessarily have to provide "equal time" for each side to present their views, though. Being fair and being balanced doesn't mean you have to present untenable, unsubstantiated, illogical and ridiculous positions or comments as being equal to reasonable, substantiated, logical and defensible positions or comments. It simply means that you try to provide audience members with as much information as you can to help them make up their own minds about which positions and comments they want to trust. In your efforts to validate and confirm information, if you discover that allegations are weak and without much merit, you should say so. Don't leave audience members with a false impression that all sides in a controversial issue have equally strong positions if they don't.

Part of being fair is being thorough in your presentation of information. Provide enough facts, figures and background information to help audience members understand the meaning and significance of issues and events. Include information that will help audience members put developments in proper perspective. Help them see connections, ramifications and implications. Give them what they need to strengthen or modify their beliefs, attitudes, values and behaviors.

Stop and Write

List and discuss five tips for avoiding ethical problems in radio-TV newswriting.

1.

2.

3.

4.

5.

Ethical Decision-Making

Radio-TV newswriters regularly confront ethical dilemmas. In order to facilitate prompt and appropriate responses, it is useful to employ an ethical decision-making model to help you sort through the issues and decide on a course of action. The following abbreviated model is one that works in a variety of settings:

1. *Determine the particulars of the situation*. Who's involved and what's involved? What's at stake? Gather facts, figures.

2. *Determine what laws or ethical guidelines apply*. Consult with attorneys and ethics codes—Radio-Television News Directors Association's Code of Ethics, the Society of Professional Journalists' Code of Ethics and/or your station's code of ethics.

3. *Determine what ethical principles and theories apply*. Among the traditional principles are truth-telling, independence, protecting the public interest, trying not to harm people and trying to make the world a better place. Among the traditional theories are trying to find a middle ground between extremes (Golden Mean), treating others the way you would want them to treat you (Golden Rule), treating everybody the same no matter who they are (Veil of Ignorance), doing whatever maximizes the good for the greatest number of people (Utilitarianism) and doing the "right" thing no matter what the consequences (Categorical Imperative).

4. *Analyze alternatives*. Explore a variety of responses and think through what the consequences of each alternative might be. Who will be helped and who will be harmed?

5. *Determine what journalists normally do in similar situations*. Try to find out what the traditional, "accepted" courses of action are and have been. Consult research studies and anecdotal accounts of what journalists believe to be correct and what they do when confronted with ethical dilemmas.

6. *Decide how you might justify your actions*. Think about the arguments you would use to convince others that you've done the right thing or at least the best thing.

7. *Do the right thing*. Take action. Too often ethical dilemmas have a tendency to paralyze journalists. After thinking about what's involved, what laws and guidelines apply, what principles and theories seem appropriate, what your alternatives are and what journalists normally do in similar situations, do something. Make a choice. Make an informed and reasoned choice.

PRACTICE ETHICAL DECISION-MAKING. Making quick and effective use of the ethical decision-making model above or any other model takes practice. You need to think about what you would do if confronted with an ethical dilemma. Think through your options. Analyze potential situations and consequences. Run through a variety of scenarios. Sound ethical decision-making cannot take place in a vacuum. Practice often enough until you are comfortable with the model. Practice often enough until ethical decision-making becomes second nature to you.

Stop and Write

Develop your own model for ethical decision-making in radio-TV newswriting. Include at least five steps.

1.

2.

3.

4.

5.

6.

7.

Broadening Your Horizons

Read as many of the following books as you can. They will help you become more proficient at ethical decision-making. They'll help you become a better journalist and mass communicator, too.

Jay Black, Bob Steele and Ralph Barney, *Doing Ethics in Journalism*
Elliot D. Cohen, *Philosophical Issues in Journalism*
Louis A. Day, *Ethics in Media Communications*
Everette E. Dennis and John C. Merrill, *Media Debates*
Deni Elliott, *Responsible Journalism*
Conrad C. Fink, *Media Ethics*
Tom Goldstein, *The News at Any Cost*
H. Eugene Goodwin, *Groping for Ethics in Journalism*
Carl Hausman, *Crisis of Conscience*
Carl Hausman, *The Decision-Making Process in Journalism*
John L. Hulteng, *The Messenger's Motives*
John L. Hulteng, *Playing It Straight*
James A. Jaksa and Michael S. Pritchard, *Communication Ethics*
Edmund B. Lambeth, *Committed Journalism*
Val E. Limburg, *Electronic Media Ethics*
Philip Meyer, *Ethical Journalism*
Jeffrey Olen, *Ethics in Journalism*
Philip Patterson and Lee Wilkins, *Media Ethics*
William L. Rivers and Cleve Mathews, *Ethics for the Media*
K. Tim Wulfemeyer, *The News Blues*

• REVIEW

1. Be sure the information you include in stories is accurate and true.

2. Libel law is ever-changing. Lately, relatives of defamed people have been allowed to sue to recover damages for pain and suffering.

3. Individuals or small groups of people can be libeled. Large groups cannot be libeled.

4. If you use the word *alleged* as an adjective, it's no legal protection.

5. Private people who think they've been libeled have to prove publication, identification, defamation and negligence (falsity). Public officials and public figures must prove all of the same things, plus malice.

6. Defenses in libel cases include truth, privilege and fair comment and criticism.

7. A person's privacy can be invaded in four main ways: intruding on physical solitude, revealing embarrassing personal facts, misappropriating someone's likeness or endorsement and placing a person in a false light in the public's eye.

8. Newsworthiness is the best defense in an invasion of privacy lawsuit.

9. Facts cannot be copyrighted. It is the writing style associated with the presentation of facts that can be copyrighted.

10. The "Doctrine of Fair Use" in copyright includes determining the purpose of the use, the amount used, the effect on the market for the original work and the public's right/need to know.

11. Do your own work. Rewrite source copy in your own words.

12. It pays to be ethical. Practice the "Golden Rule."

13. Don't sensationalize. Play it straight.

14. Strive for fairness and balance in stories.

15. Employ ethical decision-making models to help solve ethical dilemmas. Practice "doing ethics" on a regular basis.

P A R T   3

Radio-TV Newswriting Exercises

- **STYLE TEST 1**

Write the following in correct KCTI news style. Assume each item appears in the middle of a sentence. If an item is already in correct style, place an **X** in the blank.

1. 15% _____

2. 1,800 _____

3. $1,750,000 _____

4. Six-hundred-37 _____

5. Five o'clock p.m. _____

6. Nov. 8 _____

7. 964 _____

8. 8¢ _____

9. Five-thousand-five-hundred-twenty-five _____

10. Nine _____

- ## STYLE TEST 2

Write the following in correct KCTI news style. Assume each item appears in the middle of a sentence. If an item is already in correct style, place an **X** in the blank.

1. 6% _____

2. 1,000 _____

3. $6.2 million _____

4. 3-hundred-92 _____

5. 7:15 this morning _____

6. Aug. 9 _____

7. 471 _____

8. 24¢ _____

9. 9-thousand-222 _____

10. Eighteen _____

● STYLE TEST 3

Rewrite the following in correct KCTI news style. Assume each item appears in the middle of a sentence. If an item is already in correct style, place an **X** in the blank.

1. 2,000 lbs. _____

2. twelve in. _____

3. 3 ft. _____

4. 16 oz. _____

5. 55 MPH _____

6. one gal. _____

7. one-hundred yds. _____

8. 627 mi. _____

9. sixteen mm _____

10. 2 ltr. _____

• STYLE TEST 4

Write the following in correct KCTI news style. Assume each item appears in the middle of a sentence. If an item is already in correct style, place an **X** in the blank.

1. James D. Miller, 45 _____

2. 1351 South Dakota Rd. _____

3. Lt. Katrina P. Rosario _____

4. FBI _____

5. E. 42 St. _____

6. Prof. Kirsten L. Anderson, 61 _____

7. 594-2709 _____

8. Sgt. Steven S. Chow _____

9. 875 Central Blvd. _____

10. Marilyn M. Mix, 21, 6003 N. 79 Ave. _____

● STYLE TEST 5

Rewrite the following sentences in correct KCTI news style. The sentences are not necessarily story leads.

1. If the 5% cut is made, ten of the two-hundred employees would be terminated.

2. The winner was Allan E. Noh, 56, 1254 E. 95 St.

3. Enrique C. Rodriguez, head of the judging committee, reported the vote was sixteen-twelve in favor of the motion.

4. The winning run was driven in by Howard D. Jackson.

5. Midcity University was awarded the $1,006,500 grant from the Ford Foundation to conduct environmental research.

6. The sales tax increase would bring in $5.8 million, Mayor Moore exclaimed.

7. It is possible we will not have the new buses by the end of next month, according to Supervisor Maria A. Sanchez.

8. Sgt. April J. Stevens is the first female MP at Ft. Madison.

9. Atty. Terence P. Shippen, 45, 2892 Boston Ave., is a member of the NAACP.

10. The damage to the hotel was estimated at $400,000 by Fire Capt. Linda M. Smith.

- **STYLE TEST 6**

Rewrite the following sentences in correct KCTI news style. The sentences are not necessarily story leads.

1. The new plant will employ 1,800 people, Mayor Moore promised.

2. The fire was caused by a short circuit, Fire Capt. Robt. C. Tinker proclaimed.

3. Over thirty percent of all Americans fail to get enough exercise, according to researchers at Harvard University.

4. The cost of the new museum is projected to be $14,990,750 by Gov. Sorenson.

5. The NCAA asked the FBI to help in the investigation.

6. Jack D. Shelley, a professor of journalism at Midcity University, has been named as a special consultant to the FCC.

7. The two women got away with $151,250, Ellen F. Warner, president of Midcity National Bank, announced.

8. Lt. Eric B. Overton will be the speaker at the ROTC luncheon today.

9. Doris E. Williams, 72, 1930 Virginia Rd., was named "Grandma of the Year" today by the Midcity Seniors Club.

10. Juan R. Lopez, pres. of Midcity Community College, announced today that he will retire from the college on June 21.

● STYLE TEST 7

Rewrite the following sentences in correct KCTI news style. The sentences are not necessarily story leads.

1. The cost of the new building will be $6,250,000, said Midcity Public Works Dir. Norman L. Tupperman.

2. Nancy C. Holtzman, 29, 8753 N. Madison Ave., was arrested by Sgt. Sheila Y. Yang.

3. The problem is exacerbated by using cheap gasoline, mechanic Gary M. Burns announced.

4. A total of 7 persons will share the lottery jackpot of $19,000,000.

5. "Prof. Gilbert M. Wyatt is the worst instructor on campus," Prof. Ruth T. Tyler proclaimed.

6. Dr. Rachel W. Stein announced that approximately 29% of all joggers suffer from the disease.

7. Wearing an attractive green dress, Sally B. Long, pres. of Midcity Furniture, Inc., declared the thirty-first annual convention of the National Freedom League in session at 8:00 a.m.

8. Gov. Sorenson will not attend the "Candidates Forum" at 7:00 p.m. at the Midcity Convention Center.

9. The Midcity Marathon will be run on Sept. 22, Mayor Moore stated.

10. The victim suffered multiple contusions, lacerations and abrasions, Dep. Coroner Patricia S. Randolph pronounced.

• STYLE TEST 8

Rewrite the following sentences in correct KCTI news style. The sentences are not necessarily story leads.

1. Sylvia P. Davis, 29, 1783 Vista Grande Rd., has been selected as the new Dir. of the Midcity Convention and Visitors Bureau by Mayor Moore.

2. It looks like your water bills will be going up $9.50 per month starting next month.

3. Midcity paid $2,300,000 to maintain and clean city parks last year, according to a report released today by Supervisor Roger V. Hedgeman.

4. Kenneth W. Warren, 48, finished 1st and his son, Mark R. Warren, 22, finished 32 in the Midcity Midnight Walkathon.

5. Dr. Zachary M. Scott, 56, a prof. of music at Midcity University, was awarded today a $250,000 grant by the J. Donald Washburn Foundation to conduct research with gifted teen-aged musicians.

6. David D. Muller, 31, 4981 Western Blvd., was selected as Midcity Police Officer of the Year last night.

7. The last day to file your property tax payment without penalty has been extended to July 31, according to Midcity Tax Assessor Sharon A. Ishida.

8. Monica Lisa Woodward, 45, 736 Canyon Ln., died in the crash, reported Midcity Police Lt. David E. Lopez.

9. The kickoff has been moved to 6:05 p.m. to accommodate ESPN, Midcity University Athletic Dir. Melissa J. Rodriguez stated.

10. The concoction included the following: ice cream, fifteen gals; almonds, 2 lbs.; whipped cream, thirty-two oz.; and bananas, ten lbs.

● **BRIEFS 1**

Rewrite the following in correct KCTI news style.

1. (MIDCITY)—Scott F. Queen, 56, the White House photographer for former President George W. Bush, has been appointed to the State Board of Industrial Review by Gov. John B. Sorenson. Queen will be in charge of the photography section.

2. (MIDCITY)—A $3.25 million cancer research grant has been awarded to the Midcity University School of Medicine, according to Dr. Theodore N. Beeman, dean of the school. The money was awarded by the Burton P. Maxwell Foundation.

3. (MIDCITY)—Marshall James Marks, 6, died early today when he fell under the front wheels of a school bus, the Midcity coroner's office reported. Witnesses said the boy, son of Mr. and Mrs. James T. Marks, 1095 Mountain View Dr., started running along a curb as the bus approached, slipped and lost his balance.

4. (MIDCITY)—Peter B. King, 44, Martin C. Krumm, 29, and Gregory L. Loo, 37, who Midcity police believe are suspects in 12 murders in various Midwest states, were arrested today at 7:15 a.m. in an apartment at 2865 49th St. The trio of murder suspects will be arraigned this afternoon.

5. (MIDCITY)—A United Airlines jet with 109 persons aboard, including the Midcity University varsity basketball team, made a safe landing at Midcity Municipal Airport last night with one of its three engines shut down, airport officials reported. An airline spokesperson said the jet had just taken off when a fire warning light came on. There was no fire, however, just a malfunction in the light's electrical system.

● BRIEFS 2

Rewrite the following in correct KCTI news style.

1. (NEW YORK)—After a prolonged bout with liver cancer, Admiral Walter N. Hyde, ret., 71, former commander of the Atlantic Fleet Submarine Force, died here today at Memorial General Hospital. Hyde won numerous military awards, citations and commendations during the Vietnam conflict.

2. (LOS ANGELES)—Dr. Doris M. Wolf, 49, a professor of chemistry at Midcity University, was injured in a two-car traffic accident here today. She suffered multiple fractures to her left leg, but is in satisfactory condition, according to doctors at the Harbor Medical Center.

3. (AMES, Iowa)—A grain elevator exploded here this morning sending bits of metal flying as far away as 2,600 feet. Five persons were killed and 25 others were injured in the explosion. The cause of the explosion has not been determined.

4. (LAS VEGAS)—Fire destroyed part of the fashionable Desert Oasis Hotel here this morning. No one was killed, but five firefighters were injured when a ceiling collapsed on them. Among the 500 persons who had to be evacuated from the hotel was Ronald R. Moore, mayor of Midcity. Mayor Moore was here attending the National Conference of Mayors. The cause of the fire has not been determined.

5. (WASHINGTON, D.C.)—Susan L. Morton, chairwoman of the Midcity Board of Supervisors, said today reorganization of the federal bureaucracy would permit counties and cities to save time and money in applying for federal grants. Chairwoman Morton expressed her views here today in meetings before a Senate subcommittee examining government red tape. There are too many unnecessary forms and steps in the grant application processes, Chairwoman Morton claims.

● BRIEFS 3

Rewrite the following in correct KCTI news style.

1. (MIDCITY)—Harold L. Kettner, 47, was sworn in this morning as the new police chief of Midcity. Kettner, a native of Midcity and a 25-year veteran of the Midcity Police Department, replaces Bobby Joe Gray, 55, who resigned last month after suffering a heart attack.

2. (HONOLULU)—Two persons, the pilot and co-pilot, died in a plane crash near here yesterday during war games. A twin-engine 414 leased by the Pentagon crashed into a hillside shortly after takeoff, according to a spokesperson at Hickam Air Force Base. The names of the victims, the only people on board the plane, were not released.

3. (MIDCITY)—An executive order declaring Midcity a disaster area in the wake of last week's flooding was signed late last night by Gov. John B. Sorenson. Homeowners who must rebuild their damaged homes will now be eligible for low-interest loans from the state.

4. (SANTA ANA, Calif.)—Leonard P. Dunn, 53, an unemployed, disabled veteran, who has won three major consumer promotion games in the last ten years, won $25,000 yesterday from McDonald's. "I'm going to buy a new car and pay off some bills," said Dunn. Dunn's third win came when he bought a 89-cent soft drink at a McDonald's near his home here and correctly matched up four pictures on a game board.

5. (ST. LOUIS)—Using huge tank trucks and elaborate vacuumlike machines, work crews labored all night last night to clean up crude oil that poured into a southeast Missouri creek from a burst oil pipeline. Oil was floating up to four-inches deep over a three-mile stretch of Asher Creek following the accident yesterday morning, authorities said. Officials expect cleanup operations to last at least three more days.

● BRIEFS 4

Rewrite the following in correct KCTI news style.

1. (MIDCITY)—0.5%. It does not sound like much, but it can make a big difference for prospective buyers—maybe $100 per month. The 0.5% is how much Midcity Bank reduced its home mortgage rate today. The rate had been 9.25%, but now it stands at 8.75%. Other local banks are expected to replicate Midcity Bank's action.

2. (HONOLULU)—Martin B. Boyd, 68, an actor who starred in a long-running role as Dr. Lester Leland in the TV daytime drama, "All My Troubles," died here today in Sharpe Memorial Hospital. Boyd, who played the wise, but quirky doctor for 25 years, was born in Midcity. Boyd had been ill for several months with liver cancer.

3. (LOUISVILLE)—Robert J. Schroeder, 57, the world's one-hundredth artificial heart recipient, suffered a stroke last night, officials at Humana Hospital here reported. "We don't think there is any permanent damage, but we will not know for sure for at least another twenty-four hours," stated Dr. Allan M. Landers, the doctor who performed the heart replacement surgery on Schroeder last month. "Mr. Schroeder is in stable condition and resting comfortably," Landers added.

4. (MIDCITY)—Two suspects in a bank robbery in which 9 persons were shot and two were killed were arrested at a downtown hotel at 4:00 a.m. this morning, Midcity Police Public Information Officer David M. Cohen reported today at a news conference. The suspects, Randolph L. Smith, 29, and Marvin W. Chang, 31, have been charged with seven counts of attempted murder, one count of robbery and two counts of murder. The robbery occurred at the downtown branch of Midcity National Bank last Friday.

5. (MIDCITY)—Helen K. Seinfeld, 55, the current Pres. of Michigan State University in East Lansing, MI., has been selected from over one-hundred candidates by the Midcity University Board of Trustees to become the new Pres. of Midcity University, according to L. Lawrence Washington, chr. of the Board of Trustees. Seinfeld, who will assume her new post on July 1, will be paid $135,000 in base salary, but will receive a benefits package including a house, medical, dental and life insurance worth a reported $28,000 per year. Seinfeld will replace Philip A. Longley, 63, who is retiring.

● RADIO READER 1

Rewrite the following in correct KCTI news style. (TRT :15)

(MIDCITY)—Two men were killed early this morning when their car, a late model Pontiac, ran off Ruffin Ave. and flipped over, according to a Midcity police spokesperson.

The names of the men have not been released pending notification of next of kin.

Police said they suspect the driver of the car swerved to avoid something in the road, because there were 55-feet of skid marks leading to the spot where the car left the road.

"The driver obviously just lost control of the car and couldn't keep it on the road," Sgt. Rhonda S. Sanders said.

The fatalities were the 94th and 95th automobile-related deaths in the city this year so far.

● RADIO READER 2

Rewrite the following in correct KCTI news style. (TRT :15)

(MIDCITY)—A 43-year-old resident of a downtown hotel was stabbed to death today after an argument with another resident, police reported. The stabbing occurred in an alley behind the Davenport Hotel.

The victim, Lance M. Farley, of the Davenport Hotel, 206 Market St., was stabbed eleven times in the chest and back, Dep. Coroner Jack Q. Larken said.

A suspect, Franklin W. Smith, Jr., 46, also a resident of the Davenport Hotel, was arrested and charged with murder. He is being held in county jail.

The two men argued about a debt Farley owed Smith, witnesses said. The debt was reportedly $20.

● RADIO READER 3

Rewrite the following in correct KCTI news style. (TRT :15)

(MIDCITY)—Melissa W. Knight, 21, 10511 N. Pearl Ave., has been chosen "Homecoming Queen" at Midcity University. In addition to beauty, Miss Knight was chosen for her scholastic achievement and involvement in community and campus activities. Miss Knight is majoring in elementary education. She is a senior.

Miss Knight has a 3.4 GPA and serves as Vice-President of Kappa Alpha, a women's scholastic honorary society. With the selection, Miss Knight receives a $1,000 scholarship from the Associated Students of Midcity University, the student governmental organization.

● RADIO READER 4

Rewrite the following in correct KCTI news style. (TRT :15)

(MIDCITY)—A fire that fire investigators believe was intentionally set caused an estimated $85,000 damage to a vacant house in Southeast Midcity last night. A "considerable amount" of flammable fluid was used to ignite the blaze, according to Fire Capt. Carolyn C. Klinehorst.

Two persons were reported near the structure shortly before the fire broke out at 10:20 p.m. The pair left the area in a brown pickup truck that sped off at a high rate of speed, a witness reported.

Michael N. Francis and Jane T. Keever, both firefighters, were injured during firefighting efforts. They were treated at Midcity General Hospital for minor burns on their arms and hands, Klinehorst said. The injured firefighters are reported to be in satisfactory condition, Klinehorst added.

● RADIO READER 5

Rewrite the following in correct KCTI news style. (TRT :30)

(MIDCITY)—Police today are still seeking three young persons who allegedly shot and killed a Midcity woman late yesterday after spray-painting gang graffiti on the woman's home.

The victim, Mrs. Gloria E. Yates, 51, 3620 Vista Ave., was struck in the throat and upper chest by bullets, said Midcity Police Det. Curtis R. Ring.

Mrs. Yates' husband, Frederick H. Yates, 53, declined to discuss the incident with reporters.

The couple was reportedly awakened about 11:40 p.m. last night by laughs and shouts coming from the exterior wall surrounding their home. While Mr. Yates was getting dressed to go outside, Mrs. Yates went to the bathroom window and looked out. Apparently, words were exchanged and then several shots rang out.

When Mr. Yates returned to the bathroom, he found his wife bleeding and lying on the floor.

Police believe an automatic weapon was used.

The phrase "Outlaws Rule" was written on the wall.

"There is such a gang in the Midcity area," Det. Ring said, "but we do not have any evidence at this time that confirms that gang members were responsible for the shooting."

No other homes or walls in the area were painted last night and there is no indication of why the Yates' home was singled out for the spray-painting, according to Det. Ring.

• RADIO READER 6

Rewrite the following in correct KCTI news style. (TRT :30)

(MIDCITY)—Three persons wearing motorcycle helmets and black leather jackets robbed the Midcity National Bank branch office at 1708 Garth Ave. at 10:27 a.m. today, according to a Midcity Police Dept. spokesperson.

One of the robbers was armed with a weapon described by witnesses as a rifle or shotgun, MPD spokesperson David M. Cohen said. The trio of robbers fled the scene in a lime-green sedan, Cohen added. The amount of money taken was not disclosed.

"The three of them swooped in here like the Jesse James or Billy the Kid gang or somebody," Jason A. Bott, vice-president and branch manager of Midcity National Bank, exclaimed. "It was just like a scene right out of one of those old Hollywood westerns."

The bank robbery this morning is the third bank robbery in Midcity in three days. A lone robber escaped on foot with $3,750 from the Bank of Midcity branch office at 6542 Lakeland Blvd. yesterday and the Heartland Savings Bank branch office at 2312 Merton St. was robbed of $16,500 by two women two days ago.

Police have good leads for all the robberies and the investigations into the rash of bank robberies is continuing, said Cohen.

• RADIO READER 7

Write a reader story in correct KCTI news style from the following information. (TRT :30)

Fire at a "Tastee Donuts" store, 2358 Broadway (downtown). The shop is one of two "Tastee Donuts" shops in the downtown area.

Quote from Walter D. Anderson, capt., Midcity Fire Dept.:

"I think it started when a pot of oil boiled over on the stove. It was a hot one. The place was an inferno when we got here. We knew we couldn't save the donut shop, so we concentrated on saving the businesses on either side of it."

Donut shop damage estimate by Capt. Anderson: $250,000. The free-standing building was completely destroyed. Shops next door to the "Tastee Donuts" shop, "April's Flowers" and "Maria's Earrings and Things," sustained only minor smoke damage to exterior walls, according to Capt. Anderson.

Quote from Mildred E. Norton, 38, owner of the donut shop:

"It was my fault. All my fault. I forgot to turn off the stove when I went out back for a cigarette. The fire started and spread so quickly. There was nothing I could do."

No injuries reported.

Fire started at 4:00 a.m. this morning. Firefighters left scene at 8:00 a.m.

● RADIO READER 8

Write a reader story in correct KCTI news style from the following information. (TRT :30)

Nurses at the city's five major hospitals could strike tomorrow. The five hospitals have a total of 2,532 beds. A total of 1,113 nurses are involved.

Nurses, through their bargaining agent, the American Nurses Association, have submitted a proposal calling for 10% annual pay increases for each of the next two years.

Quote from Sandra F. Andrews, R.N., spokesperson for local ANA chapter:

"We're prepared to strike tomorrow if our proposal is not met in full by the negotiating team for the hospitals. We've gone without a raise for two years. Enough is enough. It's payback time."

The negotiating team for the hospitals is unlikely to accept the nurses' proposal and will probably counter with an offer of about 50% of what the nurses want, according to a spokesperson for the hospitals, Janice C. Zimmerman. No official word is expected from the hospitals' negotiating team for several hours.

Quote from Janice C. Zimmerman, spokesperson for the hospitals' negotiating team:

"We know our nurses work hard and they deserve higher salaries, but times are tough. We're hoping we can reach an agreeable compromise, but if we can't, we'll keep the hospitals open somehow. The people of Midcity won't be shortchanged on their health care needs."

Nurses presently make an average of $15.20 per hour at Midcity General Hospital, Midcity Memorial Hospital, Queen's Hospital, Kaiser Hospital and Midcity Children's Hospital. The average salary for nurses is $31,616 per year. If the nurses' salary demands are met, nurses will average $34,778 after one year and $38,256 after two years.

• RADIO READER 9

Write a reader story in correct KCTI news style from the following information. (TRT :45)

Latest traffic fatalities in Midcity County:

(1) Local woman killed and her husband injured in a collision involving four vehicles on Interstate 15 about 12 miles north of downtown Midcity. Sharon L. Richards, 21, was dead on arrival at Midcity General Hospital at 1:32 a.m. Her husband, Randolph J. Richards, 22, was hospitalized with contusions and lacerations. He is in satisfactory condition, according to doctors. The Richards' 1994 Ford Mustang was hit by a southbound motor home after the Richards swerved out of the northbound lanes in an effort to avoid two other cars that had collided. Nobody else was hurt in the mishap. Sharon Richards was the driver of the Ford Mustang.

(2) George Norman Lafferty, 49, was pronounced dead at the scene of a one-car accident in the 4700 block of Baily Ave. at 3:00 a.m. Lafferty was driving west when his vehicle swerved to the right, climbed a steep embankment, slipped back down and rolled over. Lafferty was thrown from the car. No one else was in the car.

(3) Donald K. Kiperts, 30, and Jane V. Kiperts, 27, his wife, passed away when their pickup truck crashed into a telephone pole in a rural area east of Midcity. They both died from multiple internal injuries, according to the Midcity Coroner's office. The accident occurred at 1:05 a.m.

The deaths bring the Midcity County traffic death toll to 99 for the year.

Addresses: Richards, 9539 Ranger Rd., Midcity
            Lafferty, 7761 Highdale Dr., Midcity
            Kiperts, 10799 Jeremy Ave., Midcity

All information about the accidents obtained from David M. Cohen, public information officer, Midcity Police Department.

● RADIO READER 10

Rewrite the following in correct KCTI news style. (TRT :45)

(MIDCITY)—School is out here for 78,110 students, but it is no vacation. Midcity Unified School District teachers are on strike. There was picketing at all 65 city elementary, junior high schools and high schools.

At issue, as usual, is money. Midcity teachers claim they are the poorest paid in the state. A check of salary schedules from the other major school districts in the state confirms their allegation.

Arlene C. Simpson, pres. of the Midcity Teachers Association (MTA), stated that her organization has asked for a 15% pay increase, but had been offered only 8%.

"The administration's offer is a joke," Simpson said today in an interview. "Even with the 15% increase, we'll still be the poorest paid teachers in the state. We'd need 20% to get out of the salary cellar."

About 2,400 of the district's 2,559 teachers did not report for work this morning, the first day of the strike. The average MUSD teacher earns $29,900 per year.

Dist. Supt. Eric A. Otterman said he hopes to reopen the schools tomorrow using administrators, teachers who refuse to strike and whatever substitutes he can find. He also stated he will reduce the school day from six hours to four hours.

"The district will not be embarrassed or pressured into paying more than it can afford," Otterman said. "We are willing to discuss reasonable salary requests, but 15% is out of the question. Even the 8% increase will tax our budget."

Simpson added that the teachers are willing to continue picketing schools and the district offices until their pay demands are met.

"We'll stay out as long as necessary to get what we rightfully deserve," Simpson stated.

A negotiation session between the district and the teachers is scheduled for 7:30 p.m. today.

● RADIO READER 11

Rewrite the following in correct KCTI news style. (TRT :45)

(MIDCITY)—A man hit by pepper spray during a violent confrontation with Midcity police officers passed away at 9:35 a.m. today after he was taken off life support, a Queen's Hospital spokesperson said.

Carl A. Heath, 37, 6194 Fiscus Ln. in Midcity, was pronounced dead at 9:35 a.m., according to Queen's Hospital spokesperson Christine E. Jefferson. An autopsy was scheduled.

Midcity police officers struggled with Heath three days ago after he resisted being handcuffed on Ronson Rd. near Fiscus Ln. The officers went to the neighborhood after receiving reports that a man matching Heath's description was knocking on doors and throwing rocks at houses, Homicide Lt. John B. Marlow said.

Heath was hit with the cayenne pepper-based spray at least once in the face, handcuffed and then placed on his stomach, Marlow said.

Officers stepped away from Heath briefly to talk to witnesses and when they returned to Heath, they discovered he had stopped breathing. Heath was released from the handcuffs and CPR was performed until paramedics arrived.

There have been 18 other cases in the state in which suspects who have been pepper-sprayed and restrained have later died, said Craig G. Kegel, a spokesperson for the American Civil Liberties Union.

The spray, in combination with drug or alcohol use, police restraint techniques and a large build, can induce fatal respiratory arrest, Kegel claimed.

Heath's death shares many of the characteristics of many of the deaths studied by the ACLU.

According to police and witness accounts, Heath appeared to be under the influence of drugs because of his erratic and irrational behavior. He was 6 feet 5 inches tall and weighed 285 pounds, a coroner's office official said.

The Midcity Police Department instructs officers to place suspects on their sides after they are restrained, not on their stomachs, Marlow stated.

● RADIO READER 12

Rewrite the following in correct KCTI news style. (TRT :30)

(LAS CRUCES, N.M.)—A funeral home here is suing Mountain Bell Telephone Co. for listing it in the Yellow Pages under "Frozen Foods—Wholesale."

The $250,000 suit by the Easy Rest Funeral Home claims Mountain Bell did not proofread the directory prior to publication and as a result, the mortuary claims, it has been "held up to public ridicule."

"We have received numerous crank calls over this," stated Jerry F. Perez, dir. of the funeral home. "Just yesterday, some wise guy asked what our special of the day was. The other day I was asked if we sold only 'aged' meat. It's been awful, a real nightmare. Business is down, too."

Officials at Mountain Bell Telephone Co. cannot understand how the mistake occurred.

"We proofread our Yellow Pages at least nine times before printing and distribution," claimed Mary K. Sparks, dir. of public relations for Mountain Bell. "I really don't know how we missed it. It was an honest mistake, though. We weren't trying to make fun of anyone or anything."

Mountain Bell plans to include an "Open Apology Letter" to the Easy Rest Funeral Home when telephone bills are sent out next month, according to Sparks.

The lawsuit over the misplaced listing is scheduled to be heard next month in a Las Cruces Superior Court.

The Easy Rest Funeral Home is owned by Eternal Slumber, Inc. of El Paso, Texas.

● RADIO READER 13

Rewrite the following in correct KCTI news style. (TRT :30)

(MIDCITY)—Reginald Z. Washington didn't need a file baked in a cake to break out of jail. All he needed was dental floss.

While cameras, guards and computer-controlled doors were keeping his fellow inmates in, Washington braided dental floss into a rope that was as thick as a computer power cord and used it to scale an 18-foot wall at the Midcity County Jail.

"I wonder how he got hold of so much dental floss," said Michelle V. McTighe, who lives near the jail. "He must have been saving the stuff for a long time."

The 5-foot-7, 150-pound Washington escaped from the recreation yard. He attached a weight to his waxed and minty cord, hurled it over the chain-link portion of the fence and used the cord to pull himself up and over the fence.

Washington, 32, remained at large this morning, nearly 24 hours after his escape. He had been awaiting trial on charges of assault and battery and armed robbery.

Exactly how much floss it takes to make a cord the size of Washington's is not known. Packages typically contain 50 or 100 yards.

"We're checking into how much floss he bought at the commissary," Midcity County Jail Administrator Michael G. Garver announced. "I find it incredible that somebody could use something that thin to make a rope. It's almost superhuman."

In the meantime, inmates will have to use toothpicks to get particles out of their teeth. Sales of floss have been suspended pending an investigation.

• RADIO READER 14

Rewrite the following in correct KCTI news style. (TRT :15)

(MIDCITY)—When David D. Dozier approached his dead father's hospital bed and grasped the man's hand, "his eyes opened and he looked at me and I almost had a stroke," Dozier said. Dozier, 44, and other relatives were told early today by Queen's Hospital officials that Daniel W. Dozier, 68, hospitalized for hip surgery, had died. The elder Dozier was not dead, of course, he was merely sleeping when his son came into his room.

Jurnine B. Smithson, a spokeswoman for Queen's Hospital, reported that a mixup in paperwork had occurred and resulted in the Dozier family being misinformed about the "death" of the elder Dozier. The Dozier family phone number was switched accidentally with that of another patient who had died, stated Smithson.

• RADIO READER 15

Rewrite the following in correct KCTI news style. (TRT :30)

(MIDCITY)—Well, it *did* beep.

Persistent beeping from a brown bag in an abandoned shopping cart early today made a security guard for the Midcity West Shopping Plaza suspicious.

The guard walked by the cart three times just to be sure she wasn't hearing things. The beeping blared on.

Courtney E. Moore called 911. The bomb squad responded. Several police officers and a bomb-sniffing dog cautiously examined the bag. The officers were told not to broadcast over their police radios, because radio transmissions can sometimes detonate explosive devices, according to Midcity Police Lt. Barbara M. Mueller.

After almost 60 minutes, authorities determined that the bag did not contain a bomb. The noise coming from the bag was made by an electronic music greeting card that had a faulty battery.

"With so many explosive devices and unexploded fireworks being found in the city lately," Mueller said, "it is easy to understand why the guard decided to alert authorities. If someone were to err in a case like this, it is better to err on the side of caution."

• RADIO READER 16

Write a reader story in correct KCTI news style from the following information. (TRT :30)

Last year, Americans doled out over $124,000,000,000 in charity, a report released today shows. Religious causes drew the largest share of donated dollars, garnering some $56,700,000,000, followed by $14,000,000,000 for education, according to the report from the American Association of Fund-Raising Counsel Trust for Philanthropy.

Martha B. Lauzen, editor of the report, stated individual donors gave the most, donating $101,800,000,000, which made up roughly 2% of the national personal income figure. Foundations gave $8,3000,000,000, and corporations gave only 4.8% of the total, approximately $6,000,000,000.

The $124,300,000,000 total made Americans the greatest givers in the world, according to Lauzen, with Britain a distant second at 33,000,000,000. The U.S. total represented a 6.4% rise in non-profit donations from last year. It was the largest total since the organization began charting charitable contributions in 1959.

According to the report, Americans also gave $11,600,000,000 for human services, $10,200,000,000 for health, $9,300,000,000 for arts and culture, $5,000,000,000 for public causes, $3,000,000,000 for environmental causes, $1,700,000,000 for international affairs and $12,600,000,000 to a variety of miscellaneous or undesignated causes.

• RADIO READER 17

Rewrite the following in correct KCTI news style. (TRT :30)

(WASHINGTON)—The Federal Reserve raised short-term interest rates today for the third time this year, sparking a sharp decline in stock and bond prices and a large increase in the rates that banks charge for many consumer loans. It was the Fed's attempt once again to slow the nation's brisk economic growth before it leads to higher inflation. The Fed acted by raising its target for the federal funds rate, which banks charge each other for overnight loans, to 5.75%, up from 5.50%.

Like the earlier increases, today's increase affected stock and bond prices and contributed to the steady rise in long-term interest rates, especially home mortgage rates. The Dow Jones industrial average fell 41.05 points to 3,620.42 and the yield on 30-year treasury bonds rose to 7.42%, up from 7.28% last week. Big banks, led by Citibank and Chemical Bank reacted by raising their prime rates a half a point, to 7.75%.

• RADIO READER 18

Rewrite the following in correct KCTI news style. (TRT :30)

(MIDCITY)—Hubley Electronics announced today that it will close its plant here and lay off 4,400 workers as part of a cost-cutting program to deal with a shrinking U.S. defense budget.

The layoffs, to occur over the next 12 months, represent nearly 10% of the aerospace firm's worldwide work force and are expected to deal a sharp blow to the Midcity economy.

"We must continue to maintain a competitive edge if we are going to develop a business base that will help us ensure a viable company and thriving work force into the future," said C. Michael Armstead, Hubley's chairman and chief executive officer.

Hubley plans to vacate 3,000,000 square feet of office and manufacturing space and sell 275 acres of South Midcity property. The land has been valued at $75,000,000.

Hubley officials indicated that some Midcity employees will be transferred to other Hubley facilities, but most will have to find work elsewhere.

● RADIO READER 19

Rewrite the following in correct KCTI news style. (TRT :30)

(MIDCITY)—An auto plant that stood vacant for more than a decade has been transformed into a retail factory where manufacturing assembly lines have been replaced by streams of shoppers hunting for bargains.

The Mega Mall of Midcity opened today. It is being hailed as the "biggest off-price shopping center in the nation." It has 214 tenants, mostly discount and outlet stores.

The mall is getting attention for more than its 1,300,000 square feet of retail space. Developers say it proves the growing popularity of discount stores and factory outlets.

"People today, no matter how much money they make, want bargains," said Wayne W. Clarke, the general manager of The Mega Mall of Midcity. "They want value. Designer labels don't mean as much as they used to."

The $100,000,000 redevelopment is 70% leased. Up to 4,000 jobs are expected to be created when the mall is at 100%. Clarke projects $350,000,000 in yearly sales at the mall.

All of the mall's 214 tenants, including fast-food establishments, have signed agreements to sell their goods at 20%-60% below retail. Anchor stores include Marshall's Superstore, Burlington Coat Factory and Sportland Team Sports, the biggest with 85,000 square feet.

● RADIO READER 20

Rewrite the following in correct KCTI news style. (TRT :30)

(WASHINGTON)—Southwest Airlines overtook American Airlines last year as the leading carrier in overall quality, a private study concluded.

"It's not so much that American performed worse," Gerald T. Tucker, dir. of the Air Travel Institute, said, "it's just that Southwest performed better."

The research, conducted by the Air Travel Institute, ranked 9 airlines with annual operating revenues of $1,000,000,000 or more on 19 factors, including on-time performance, baggage handling, how often people get bumped from flights, fares and frequent-flier programs. The factors are weighted based on customer comments on what is important to them.

Southwest, which is the nation's 7th largest air carrier in terms of passengers, ranked 1st in baggage handling, on-time percentage and in frequency of low fares, institute officials reported.

American Airlines had been ranked 1st in the first three years of the institute's surveys.

TWA showed the greatest overall improvement last year moving from last in the rankings to 7th.

In order, the overall airline rankings released today: Southwest, American, United, Delta, USAir, Northwest, TWA, America West and Continental.

● RADIO READER 21

Write a reader story in correct KCTI news style from the following information. (TRT :30)

Big high school basketball game last night. Midcity Central High School lost to Western High School 74-63. Brian T. Sawyer, a 6-foot-9 senior forward, scored 25 points and had 19 rebounds for the winning Wildcats. Mark W. Warren, a 6-foot-3 junior guard, led the way for the losing Lumberjacks with 21 points.

Team records:
> Central (11-3, overall; 4-1 league)
> Western (9-5, overall; 3-2 league)

The Lumberjacks led at halftime 40-38, but Wildcats coach Scotty K. Jordan changed from a zone to a man-to-man defense for the second half and the Wildcats rallied behind a tough, scrambling defense and some hot outside shooting.

"We put a lot of pressure on their guards in the second half," Jordan said. "Once we made it tough for them to get the ball inside, we were able to neutralize their height advantage and we just pulled away."

Wildcats 6-foot-1 sophomore guard Erik J. Wolf hit two consecutive 3-point shots midway through the 3rd quarter to put the Wildcats in the lead to stay at 51-50. Wolf finished with 22 points and 6 steals. He had 12 assists, too.

The win moves the Wildcats into a second place tie with Jefferson High School in the Central League. The Lumberjacks remain in 1st place despite their first league loss of the season.

Other scorers:
> Western (Gary C. Chow, 11; Aaron H. Webster, 9; Thomas P. Ramos, 5; John S. Saxon, 2)
> Central (Michael D. Emery, 10; Bradley J. Kamau, 9; Peter B. Mann, 8; Jorge E. Guerrero, 8; Franklin R. Chu, 7)

● RADIO READER 22

Rewrite the following in correct KCTI news style. (TRT :30)

(LOS ANGELES)—All she wanted to do was pitch. And pitch she did. She pitched her way into sports history.

Julie K. Baldwin, 18, became the first woman to pitch in an NCAA college baseball game today when she took the mound for Southern California College in a game against San Diego State University. And hers was no token appearance. The left-handed freshman started the game and she was around at the finish. In an overpowering statement for gender equity, Baldwin tossed a 7-hitter as Southern California College routed San Diego State University 12-1.

Baldwin's pitching line showed: 104 pitches, three walks and two strikeouts.

SDSU junior outfielder Mickey M. Maxwell spoiled Baldwin's shutout bid with a booming home run in the top of the 7th inning.

"I didn't sleep much last night," Baldwin said after her victory. "When I went out there, I was really shaking. I wasn't afraid, just nervous about doing my job. I just wanted to get a win for my team."

Baldwin, 5-foot-9 and 150 pounds, seemed unimpressed with becoming the first woman ever to pitch in an NCAA baseball game.

"That doesn't mean anything to me," she said. "I just enjoy being out there with a great bunch of guys."

Baldwin, who is on scholarship, played 4 years on the boys varsity baseball team at Troy High School in Fullerton, Calif., where she compiled a 16-7 overall record with an ERA of 2.31. She rang up 165 strikeouts in 147 innings.

● RADIO READER 23

Write a reader story in correct KCTI news style from the following information. (TRT :30)

Soccer match this afternoon at Midcity University. The MU women's varsity team crushed Western Mississippi State University 6-1. It was the 5th win in a row for the Lady Tigers. Junior Heather O. Ross scored twice in the game's first 16 minutes and seniors Allison F. Gandolf and Kristen L. McIntosh added goals as the Lady Tigers opened a 4-1 lead over the Lady Warriors at halftime.

Junior Rita R. Romero and Sophomore Patricia I. Tanibe scored for MU in the second half.

"We played great defense today," MU coach Jackie P. Swanson said. "We had a slight lapse near the end of the first half, but other than that, we played with intensity and confidence. We ran our offensive patterns to perfection. Western Mississippi is a good team, too. We just put it all together. It shows you what we're capable of."

Records:
Midcity University (9-4)
Western Mississippi (7-7)

MU will go against the top-rated team in the country, the University of Tennessee-Knoxville (12-0), next Tuesday in Tennessee.

"We're looking forward to the game," Swanson said. "We're on a roll right now and playing our best soccer of the year. I think we have a great chance to pull an upset."

- ## RADIO READER 24

Write a reader story in correct KCTI news style from the following information. (TRT :30)

Upset in local high school football last night. West Valley High School knocked off Roosevelt High School 24-21. The loss was the first of the year for the Roughriders and moved the West Valley High School Eagles into a first place tie with Roosevelt in the Southern League. Both teams have league records of 5-1. Overall records: Roosevelt 8-1; West Valley (6-3).

Roosevelt went into tonight's game as the top-ranked team in the city. West Valley was not ranked in the top 10.

Turnovers were the difference in the game. The Roughriders fumbled 6 times, losing 4. They also threw 3 interceptions. The Eagles suffered no turnovers.

Junior running back Sean S. Jackson rushed for 202 yards on 30 carries to lead the Eagles. He scored two touchdowns on runs of 15 and 36 yards. Quarterback Bryant W. Burke passed for 158 yards (12 for 18) and scored the other Eagles touchdown on a 3-yard run. Timothy M. Erickson kicked a 42-yard field goal and 3 extra points for the Eagles.

Senior running back Lawrence C. Chen was the offensive leader for the Roughriders. He rushed for 253 yards and scored all three touchdowns on runs of 2, 6 and 81 yards.

Next week marks the end of the regular season for both teams. If both win, they will both go into the city championship playoffs. If Roosevelt loses, it will be eliminated from the playoffs. West Valley, by virtue of its win over Roosevelt, is assured a playoff spot even if it loses next week. Roosevelt plays at home next week against Jefferson High School and West Valley travels to Mountain View High School. Both games are scheduled for 7:30 p.m. Friday.

● RADIO READER 25

Rewrite the following in correct KCTI news style. (TRT :30)

(KANSAS CITY, Mo.)—No power-play goals. No penalty killing. No intensity. No victory.

The Midcity IceStars suffered their 4th straight defeat last night thanks to a combination of just such maladies. They trailed 2-0 at the end of one period, 3-0 after two periods and 7-1 when the final horn sounded in their Midwest Hockey League game with the Kansas City Blades.

The Blades (7-1-0) got two goals and two assists from David M. Bruce and two goals and one assist from Alexi Z. Voltrov, but the real star of the night was rookie Blades goaltender Trevor M. Robin. Only a meaningless goal by IceStars forward John N. Lilley late in the 3rd period prevented Robin from garnering his 3rd shutout of the young season.

The game was easily the IceStars worst performance of the season. At least in the previous 3 losses, the IceStars (2-5-1) could point to brief stretches in each game that prevented them from winning. Last night there was not much that was positive.

"I think they really exposed some of our vulnerable areas," IceStars coach Walter P. Kyle said. "Our defensemen did not play well in one-on-one situations, we did not convert any power plays and we really stunk it up in five-on-five situations."

The IceStars return home tomorrow night to play the Oklahoma City Cowboys (3-3-2) at 7:05 p.m. at the Midcity Sports Palace.

● RADIO READER 26

Write a reader story in correct KCTI news style from the following information. (TRT :15)

Dow Jones stock report for today. 30 Industrials stocks closed at 3850.59. Down 4.71 from yesterday. High for the day was 3883.56 and low was 3803.49. 390,170,900 shares traded. Advancing stocks, 121,571,400. Declining stocks, 159,411,800. The rest unchanged.

20 Transportation stocks closed at 1474.13. Down 1.63 from yesterday. High for the day was 1484.14 and low was 1461.32.

15 Utilities stocks closed at 177.63. Up .20 from yesterday. High for the day was 179.01 and low was 175.39.

Gold selling for $389.30 per ounce. Down $.10 from yesterday.

● RADIO READER 27

Write a reader story in correct KCTI news style from the following information. (TRT :15)

Dow Jones stock report for today. 30 Industrials stocks closed at 3908.12. Down 22.54 from yesterday. High for the day was 3956.90 and low was 3889.28. 368,164,900 shares traded. Advancing stocks, 113,218,900. Declining stocks, 151,145,100. The rest unchanged.

20 Transportation stocks closed at 1526.99. Down 9.78 from yesterday. High for the day was 1545.39 and low was 1517.44.

15 Utilities stocks closed at 181.91. Down .26 from yesterday. High for the day was 182.64 and low was 180.27.

Gold selling for $391.30 per ounce. Up $1.20 from yesterday.

- ## RADIO READER 28

Write a reader story in correct KCTI news style from the following information. (TRT :15)

Weather forecast for tomorrow: A weak ridge of high pressure will bring partly to mostly sunny skies with dry conditions. A dissipating cold front will pass through the area, causing some high clouds to develop. Highs should range from 64-68. Lows will range from 52-56.

Extended forecast: Mostly cloudy with scattered showers possible the day after tomorrow. Highs will range from 66-70 and lows from 48-54.

Today's readings: High was 72 at Midcity Municipal Airport. Low expected to hit between 54-58.

Current temperature: 64.

- ## RADIO READER 29

Write a reader story in correct KCTI news style from the following information. (TRT :15)

Weather forecast for tomorrow: An upper-level high pressure system will weaken throughout the day as a cold front pushes southward across the area. As a result, temperatures will drop dramatically from today's highs and lows. Should be mostly cloudy. Highs tomorrow should range from 34-38. Lows will range from 22-26.

Extended forecast: Cloudy in the morning, but becoming partly cloudy by mid-afternoon the day after tomorrow. Highs should range from 38-42 and lows will range from 30-34.

Today's readings: High was 56. Low expected to dip to 38.

Current temperature: 48.

- ## RADIO READER 30

Write a reader story in correct KCTI news style from the following information. (TRT :15)

Almost .75 of an inch of rain has fallen so far today, according to National Weather Service forecaster Jesse M. Lee. The measurement was taken about thirty minutes ago at Midcity Municipal Airport.

"We expect at least another inch and maybe 1.50 inches more rain will fall before midnight tonight," Lee stated.

Forecast for tomorrow: Mostly cloudy with rain likely throughout the day, but rain should taper off in the evening as a high pressure system moves into the area. Highs expected to range between 72-76. Low should range between 54-58.

Extended forecast: High pressure will mean colder temperatures, but no rain. High temperatures the day after tomorrow should range between 56-60 and lows should range between 40-44.

Today's readings: High was 75. Low expected to be 62-66.

Current conditions: Rain falling. Temperature is 70.

Storm totals: .95 of rain in past 24 hours. Could be as much as 2-inches total of rainfall from storm before storm moves out of area.

● RADIO ACTUALITY STORY 1

Write an introduction and tail in correct KCTI news style from the following information for the actuality.
(TRT :30)

Lt. Carl R. Mercer, spokesperson for the Midcity Police Association (MPA), warns that local police officers will conduct a massive "sickout" next Monday to protest the Midcity Board of Supervisors' refusal to grant officers a 15% pay increase. The Board of Supervisors has offered a 10% increase.

Salary negotiations between the MPA and the Board of Supervisors were held last night, but no accord was reached. Another session is scheduled for tonight at 7:30 p.m. at the Midcity Convention Center.

Police have threatened to strike next month if pay demands aren't met.

MERCER ACTUALITY: (Time :10)
    "We have to do something to show we mean business. We just can't accept the 10%. We need the full 15% to stay competitive with other departments in the state. Right now, the average police officer in Midcity only makes $28,000 a year. It's a disgrace."

● RADIO ACTUALITY STORY 2

Write an introduction and tail in correct KCTI news style from the following information.
(TRT :30)

Here's a switch! A doctor who is trying to keep patients away. Doctor Donna Z. Loren, one of Midcity's top plastic surgeons, claims too many people come to her asking for unnecessary or impossible plastic surgery.

In order to combat this growing problem, Dr. Loren has decided to offer weekend seminars entitled "What Plastic Surgery Can and Can't Do for You." The seminars will be held from 9:00 a.m.-5:00 p.m. each Saturday for the next two months at the Midcity Inn's Regal Room.

All of the seminars will be exactly the same, so a person needs only to attend one. The seminars will be free and open to the public.

If more information is desired, it can be obtained from Dr. Loren's office. Phone number: 1-800 NEW FACE

LOREN ACTUALITY: (Time :10)
    "There's a lot of misinformation floating around concerning plastic surgery. Some people actually think we can make them look just like their favorite movie star. My seminar is designed to give people a realistic picture of what plastic surgery can and can't do."

- ## RADIO ACTUALITY STORY 3

Write an introduction and tail in correct KCTI news style from the following information for the actuality.
(TRT :30)

The Midcity Board of Supervisors has cut $325,000 from next year's budget for Midcity Childcare Centers. There are 5 centers in Midcity. The total current budget for the 5 centers is $975,000. The centers currently serve approximately 500 preschool children from low-income families.

The supervisors think the $325,000 will be better used to help support a new after-school playground program at local elementary schools.

Jane A. Reeger, dir. of Midcity Childcare Centers, is concerned about the cut. The cut means Midcity Childcare Centers will be forced to drop 150 children, she said.

REEGER ACTUALITY: (Time :10)
    "The cut is ridiculous. We provide a valuable service. We help kids get ready for school and allow parents to work or look for work. The cut will severely damage our program. That after-school program is fine, but I don't think it's as important as our program."

- ## RADIO ACTUALITY STORY 4

Write an introduction and tail in correct KCTI news style from the following information for the actuality.
(TRT :30)

Midcity Police shot and killed a woman who was holding her cat at knifepoint in a grocery store today. The woman came into the Food Basket store, 7193 W. Petrie Ave., with her Siamese cat and a knife and sat down in an aisle, said MPD Sgt. William D. Briscoe. Store employees placed rows of shopping carts at either end of the aisle, moved bystanders away and called police. When police officers arrived, they asked the woman, who has not been identified as yet, to drop the knife. With that, she began threatening to kill the cat, Briscoe said. The woman got up and began walking toward the officers, who sprayed her with pepper spray mace in an effort to halt her advance. When she didn't halt, one officer opened fire. The woman dropped the cat as she collapsed. The cat got loose in the store and has not been found. Midcity Animal Control officers were even called, but they could not locate the cat. They believe it is still in the store.

BRISCOE ACTUALITY (TIME :05)
    "She raised her knife above her head and charged the officers. It was unfortunate, but it was a clean shoot."

● RADIO WRAPAROUND STORY 1

Create a reporter wraparound in correct KCTI news style from the following information. You will be the reporter for the story. Include an introduction and tail for the newscaster. (TRT :45)

Board of Supervisors voted 7-2 at meeting today to ban smoking in all Midcity restaurants beginning June 1. City Attorney Margaret H. Adams was directed to make the necessary revisions in the city ordinances regulating restaurants.

Issue has been debated for several months. Opponents have argued that the marketplace should regulate the smoking issue, not the government. Supervisor Ricardo E. Ramos has been a vocal critic of the proposed ban. He voted against it even though he is a non-smoker.

RAMOS ACTUALITY: (Time :12)
"The marketplace should take care of things. Individual rights are key here. If a restaurant does not have an adequate separation between smoking and non-smoking sections, people should go elsewhere. If a restaurant wants to become non-smoking, it should do so on its own, not because of government regulation."

Betty B. Woodson, the owner of "Betty's Cafe," criticized the decision, too. She complained that as a businessperson, she should have the right to decide how best to run her business.

On the other side of the issue, representatives from the American Heart Association and the American Lung Association praised the decision. They stressed the importance of taking drastic measures to deal with the dangers of second-hand smoke to patrons and workers alike.

Robert C. and Mary Jo McFadden, owners of "Bobby's," a local coffee shop chain of 6 restaurants, support the ban. They say Midcity should be a leader in creating safe eating environments for all people.

A loophole in the smoking ban regulations makes it possible for restaurants to apply for a waiver from observing the ban if it can be proved that the ban is hurting business.

● RADIO WRAPAROUND STORY 2

Create a wraparound story in correct KCTI news style from the following information. You will be the reporter for the story. Include an introduction and tail for the newscaster. (TRT :45)

Officials from the Midcity Transit Board (MTB) announced at a news conference this morning that the month-old experiment of having city buses equipped with surveillance video cameras has helped reduce vandalism. The experiment consisted of 5 buses equipped with several video cameras and recording devices. The buses were used mostly on Route 7, which runs from East Midcity to the downtown area.

There was approximately 75% less vandalism on the video buses during the past month compared to the month before, according to Carmen F. Sandoval, MTB general manager.

At the news conference today, MTB officials displayed a bus that they said was typical of most in their 266-bus fleet. Most of the seats, walls and windows in the rear half of the 2-month-old, 65-foot-long bus were marred by the destructive work of vandals who had used felt-tip markers, glue sticks or glass-etching tools.

SANDOVAL ACTUALITY: (TIME :09)
> "We're very pleased with the results so far. We think the cameras will save us a lot of money in the long run and we're going to seek outside funding and grants to equip the rest of our fleet, so taxpayers won't have to foot the bill."

Damage from vandalism costs the MTB an average of $50,000 per month to repair, according to Sandoval. She predicts the cameras will cut that figure by 50% at least. It costs approximately $5,000 to equip a single bus with the necessary hardware for the "Big Brother" surveillance, according to MTB officials.

● RADIO WRAPAROUND STORY 3

Create a wraparound story in correct KCTI news style from the following information. You will be the reporter for the story. Include an introduction and tail for the newscaster. (TRT :45)

New report out from Midcity University's School of Medicine. For three months, researchers followed 373 men and women who work outside of the home and found that men with stressful jobs have higher than usual blood pressure even when they sleep, suggesting that such difficult work permanently damages their circulatory systems. The study found that working women were less likely than men to demonstrate ill effects of job stress.

Researchers hooked up volunteers to portable monitors at various times during the day and charted how their blood pressure went up or down in response to the pressures and challenges of the day. Dr. Virginia W. Eggers and Dr. Lloyd K. Hisaka found that people in highly demanding jobs with little autonomy had significantly higher blood pressures than did those in less taxing situations. Those in high-stress, low-freedom jobs had blood pressures that averaged 137 over 85, compared to 129 over 83 for other people. Normal blood pressure is 120 over 80. In all age comparison groups, women averaged 4-6 blood pressure measures lower than men with similar jobs.

HISAKA ACTUALITY: (TIME :09)
　　"No one can say for sure which came first, the job stress or the high blood pressure, but there is a clear connection.
　　It could be that people with Type A personalities already have a tendency to high blood pressure and are attracted to
　　high-stress jobs."

Hisaka added that it is clear from the study's findings that the cumulative effect of the exposure to stress over time permanently raises blood pressure.

"Having a stress buffer, such as someone at home or at work to talk to about the day's problems, seemed to help reduce blood pressure levels and ease the strain of demanding jobs," Dr. Eggers announced.

- ## RADIO WRAPAROUND STORY 4

Create a wraparound story in correct KCTI news style from the following information. You will be the reporter for the story. Include an introduction and tail for the newscaster. (TRT 1:00)

Midcity Police were looking for drug dealers, but instead found 19 children living in a 4-room apartment that was littered with filth and crawling with cockroaches this morning. The youngest child appeared to be 1 year old and the oldest was 14 years old, a police official said. Police raided the apartment at 5827 Halberns Ave. after receiving a tip about alleged drug activity, according to David M. Cohen, MPD spokesperson. Six adult relatives of the children, four mothers, a father and an uncle, were charged with felony child endangerment. Another mother of some of the children is being sought and a 6th mother is in the hospital giving birth, police reported. All of the arrested adults were taken to the Midcity County Jail. Bail was set at $100,000 for each.

Sgt. Joel A. Banks was one of the first police officers to get inside the apartment. He said one of the children, a 4 year old, had to be hospitalized, but all the others were taken to a private shelter for neglected children after they were examined at Midcity General Hospital. The 4 year old is in satisfactory condition with cigarette burns and contusions on his arms and legs.

BANKS ACTUALITY: (TIME :15)
"The only remorse they showed was when they found out they were going to be arrested. They should be ashamed of themselves. The apartment was cold, there were feces on the floor and there was garbage everywhere. It was the filthiest, most disgusting place I've ever seen."

Arrested were Linda Rae Curlee, 31; Nancy C. Brown, 27; Wanda L. Brown, 23; Anne R. Sandusky, 21; Marvin P. Sandusky, 24; and Larry S. Walker, 33.

"The injuries to the 4 year old could lead to charges of child abuse," Cohen said, "but we're waiting until we have more information from the doctors who examined him."

• RADIO VOICER STORY 1

Write an introduction and tail in correct KCTI news style from the following information for the voicer. (TRT :45)

About 125 postal workers picketed this morning outside the U.S. Post Office in downtown Midcity, 1284 Main St. Most carried signs. There was no confrontation, just a lot of angry shouting and name calling by both sides—workers and management—but police were called to the scene by management. Police officers just watched from across the street. They never got involved. Negotiations to end the 5-day strike are scheduled to resume in Washington, D.C., tomorrow. A local spokesperson for the U.S. Postal Service reported that mail will continue to be delivered as usual by nonstriking personnel and management personnel.

Reporter Tim Daniels produced a :30 voicer on the demonstration. None of the above information is included in his voicer.

DANIELS VOICER IN:
"The picketers are upset about the overtime hours that they're forced to work."

DANIELS VOICER OUT:
"Tim Daniels for KCTI radio news."

DANIELS VOICER TAPE TIME: :30

• RADIO VOICER STORY 2

Write an introduction and tail in correct KCTI news style from the following information for the voicer. (TRT :45)

The Midcity Board of Supervisors has approved the purchase of two adjacent parcels of land in the downtown area on which to build the Midcity Cultural Center. The parcels are located at the corner of Broadway and Main Streets. The purchase price was a combined $1,576,000.

The purchase includes $827,000 for a 28,908 sq. ft. parcel owned by Shipstad Restaurants, Inc., and $749,000 for a 25,700 sq. ft. parcel owned by Midcity Federal Savings Bank.

The proposed 3-story Midcity Cultural Center has been in the planning stages for 3 years. It will house a museum, gift shop, restaurant and a theater.

Reporter Brenda Dunn produced a :30 voicer on the purchase. None of the above information is included in her voicer.

DUNN VOICER IN:
"The two pieces of land complete the initial stage of the plans for the cultural center."

DUNN VOICER OUT:
"Brenda Dunn for KCTI radio news."

DUNN VOICER TAPE TIME: :30

● RADIO VOICER STORY 3

Write an introduction and tail in correct KCTI news style from the following information for the voicer. (TRT 1:00)

A new program will begin next semester at Midcity University. The program is designed to help students learn to read better. It will feature 5 classes, each with 25 students each semester for one year. Students will be eligible for the special reading improvement classes if they score below 70% on the university's reading competency entrance test that is given to all incoming freshmen.

Money to fund the new program will come from a $125,000 grant awarded to Dr. Robert A. Scott, professor of English at MU, by the National Humanities Institute. The program will be run on an experimental basis for two semesters. If it is judged successful by the university administration, it will likely be made a permanent part of the MU curriculum, according to Dr. Scott.

In the last freshman class, 25% of the frosh failed to reach the 70% level on the reading competency test, Dr. Scott reported. Dr. Scott said he feels a score of 70% is necessary for a person to be considered an average adult reader.

Reporter Mike James produced a :30 voicer on the new program. He filed his report from the university. None of the above information is included in his voicer.

JAMES VOICER IN:
"MU officials hope the program will help freshmen do better in school."

JAMES VOICER OUT:
"Mike James for KCTI radio news."

JAMES VOICER TAPE TIME: :30

● RADIO VOICER STORY 4

Write an introduction and tail in correct KCTI news style from the following information for the voicer. (TRT 1:00)

Professional fund-raisers raised nearly $31,000,000 for charity in Midcity last year, but kept 66.34% of the money, according to a report by the Midcity City Attorney.

Two out of every three dollars donated by Midcity residents to charities which used commercial fund-raisers did not go to charity at all, City Attorney Margaret H. Adams stated, but instead went to solicitation expenses and to fund-raiser profits.

Adams reported she does not want to discourage Midcity residents from giving to charities that need the money, but she hoped to encourage people to ask questions about who is collecting the donations and what they do with the money they collect.

Adams announced at a morning news conference that she will continue to monitor the activities of professional fund-raisers in Midcity to ensure they follow regulations and fully disclose to donators the precise percentage of their donations that actually goes to the advertised charity.

Reporter Sharon Estrada created a :40 voicer on the fund-raising story. She filed her report from city hall.

ESTRADA VOICER IN:
"Adams says most of the professional fund-raisers don't do anything illegal, but many are unethical."

ESTRADA VOICER OUT:
"From City Hall, I'm Sharon Estrada, KCTI Radio News."

ESTRADA VOICER TAPE TIME: :40

● RADIO LIVE REPORT (ROSR) 1

Write an introduction in correct KCTI news style from the following information for the ROSR. (TRT :40)

Reporter Greg Sampson is live at the Midcity Convention Center. He will report on the start of the Beer Can Collectors Association's annual convention. First time the convention has ever been held in Midcity. Over 5,000 registrants are participating. Convention will run for three days.

Convention is open to the public and there are more than 2,500 separate collections on display.

Sampson will attempt to walk around the display area and talk about some of the more unusual cans.

Sampson will get :30, so the introduction should run :10.

● RADIO LIVE REPORT (ROSR) 2

Write an introduction in correct KCTI news style from the following information for the ROSR. (TRT :40)

Reporter Christina Noriega is live outside the chambers of the Midcity Board of Supervisors. The Supervisors have just completed a vote on whether to eliminate free parking at the Midcity Zoo. This is a "hot button" issue in Midcity. There have been public hearings and debates for months. The community seems about evenly split on the issue.

Noriega has been following the story from the start. She will give the results of the vote and summarize the comments of some of the Supervisors.

Noriega will get :30, so the introduction should run :10.

● RADIO LIVE REPORT (ROSR) 3

Write an introduction in correct KCTI news style from the following information for the ROSR. (TRT 1:00)

Reporter Brett Draper is live at the scene of a traffic accident involving a Midcity Unified School District bus and a Toyota pickup truck. Police report that two people in the truck and a dog riding in the back of the truck are dead and 14 children in the bus are injured. Accident occurred at the corner of Westminster Blvd. and Valley Vista Rd. Accident occurred about 20 minutes ago.

Draper will give the details known about the accident and information for what parents can do to get information about their children.

Draper will get :45 for his report, so the introduction should run :15.

● RADIO LIVE REPORT (ROSR) 4

Write an introduction in correct KCTI news style from the following information for the ROSR. (TRT 1:00)

Reporter Sheena Edwards is live at the scene of a fire at an apartment building at 4686 Winona St. Fire officials don't think there are any fatalities, but the fire is still burning. The building houses an estimated 220 persons. The first fire alarm sounded just eight minutes ago. Edwards was in a KCTI news car near the apartment building when she heard the report on her police/fire scanner. She was returning to the station from an assignment to report on a fire safety seminar at Midcity Central High School.

Edwards will describe what's going on and summarize what are the best guesses of fire officials about how long the fire might continue to burn.

Edwards will get :45 for her report, so the introduction should run :15.

● RADIO NEWSCAST 1

1-A

(MIDCITY)—A Midcity-based consumer group, the Environmental Protection Organization (EPO), asked the federal government today to ban the sale of children's sleepwear containing the widely used fire retardant called "Tris," because it claims there is a "significant cancer hazard" connected with the use of Tris.

"Nearly 100% of garments made of 100% polyester fabrics have been treated with Tris," Dr. William P. Bates, an EPO research chemist, stated at a morning news conference.

"We have some data that suggest that Tris, which sometimes amounts to 10% of the weight of a treated garment, can be absorbed through the skin or it can be ingested if a child sucks or chews on the garment," Bates pronounced.

Apparently, washing a garment that is treated with Tris significantly reduces the amount of the chemical, although not all of it is eliminated, according to Bates.

1-B

(DEMING, N.M.)—A motorist on Interstate 10 near here had an unusual explanation for two New Mexico State Highway Patrol officers when he was stopped for weaving yesterday.

Glenn G. Baxter, Jr., told the officers his pet boa constrictor had gotten out of its cage and was slithering around in the car.

Officer Marc P. Waxton and Officer Ronald S. Morren helped Baxter recapture the snake, but apparently the officers provided the assistance with varying degrees of enthusiasm.

"Waxton says it (the snake) was 6 feet long, but he's afraid of snakes," Morren said. "I say it was only 4 feet long, but then I'm not afraid of snakes."

Baxter was not cited.

1-C

(MIDCITY)—Charles O. Sennett, 24, 7621 Ramsgate Blvd., Midcity, died last night when his motorcycle collided with a pickup truck on Magnolia Avenue. Sennett lost control of his Honda motorcycle, crossed over the center stripe and rammed into the oncoming Nissan pickup truck, Midcity Police Department Public Information Officer David M. Cohen reported. Sennett was pronounced dead on arrival at Midcity General Hospital.

Pamela T. Nater, 19, 44965 Haver St., Midcity, the driver of the pickup truck, was not injured or cited in the 11:50 p.m. accident.

1-D

(DES MOINES, Iowa)—Wives and husbands may enter voting booths together, a State Administrative Law Judge ruled here today.

"The law is constitutional and must be followed," Judge John F. Edwards said after reviewing the Iowa Conjugal Voting Bill, AB10985.

Edwards said the law did not violate the "secret ballot" concept, which he called "sacred to all true Americans."

Iowa Election Commission Chairperson Karen L. Caster said she would instruct all Iowa counties to obey the law, but she asked, "What's the difference between husband and wife voting together and brother and sister, or boyfriend and girlfriend, or even employer and employee?"

The Iowa law also allows a voter to request assistance in voting from a poll watcher or official.

1-E

(MIDCITY)—Two men, one armed with a sawed-off shotgun, robbed a clothing store here of approximately $2,517 in cash and two $250 suits last night, police reported.

The robbery occurred shortly before 11:00 p.m. at Martin's Merchantile, 1722 Highland Ave., Lt. Gregory J. Craig said.

Teri A. Dantly, a saleswoman at the store, said the men entered the store and selected two suits from the racks. As she wrote up the bill, one of the men pulled a shotgun and demanded the suits and all the money in the cash register.

Four customers and two other sales personnel were in the store at the time of the robbery, according to Dantly. All seven of them were ordered into dressing rooms and they remained there until the robbers had made their escape.

Martin's Merchantile was having an all-night sale at the time of the robbery.

The robbers were described as two clean-shaven Caucasian men, between 30 and 40 years old, with long hair. Police have no suspects in custody.

1-F

NEWS RELEASE

M	U
S	D

Midcity Unified School District   4100 Normal Street, Midcity
Miles M. Milburn, Director of Public Information
(800) 444-4444

FOR IMMEDIATE RELEASE   FOR IMMEDIATE RELEASE

TEST SCORES LEVEL OFF IN CITY SCHOOLS

The annual decline in Midcity Unified School District comparative test scores may have ebbed for the first time in over a decade, the Board of Education was told today. The results of last year's testing of grades 6, 8, and 10 pupils show the scores held steady in comparison with scores from the year before after over ten years of decline, said Dr. Karl R. Ester, director of the district's evaluation services.

"I'm not saying that we have solved our problems, but this is a most encouraging sign," said Ester.

The students took the Comprehensive Test of Basic Skills, which Ester described as the most widely used test in the country. Each of the three grades was tested in seven areas, giving 21 points of comparison between the average student last year and the year before. Sixteen of the comparison points showed exactly the same position relative to the year before, three points showed improved positions and two points showed slight declines.

"It's really a super performance by our kids," Ester said. "And, of course, we continue to score well above the national norms."

Taking the average student in the nation as the one who scores at the 50th percentile rank, Midcity students scored above the national average in 20 of the 21 comparison points. The only area below the national average was 6th grade spelling, the report showed.

#####

1-G

(MIDCITY)—Three Midcity Board of Supervisors members maneuvered wheelchairs through an obstacle course this afternoon in observance of the first day of the annual Midcity Handicapped Awareness Week.

James K. Bates, Susan L. Morton and Roger V. Hedgeman joined other city officials to dramatize the obstacles handicapped people face each day, such as curbs, unevenly textured ground and incorrectly constructed ramps. The event took place at the Rehabilitation Institute of Midcity.

"It opens your eyes," Morton said. "We have to be sure we're doing all we can to make access and opportunities equal for all our citizens."

1-H

(MIDCITY)—$.08. That's how much the price of milk (per half gallon) has dropped in the Midcity area since the state decontrolled minimum retail prices last Thursday. MIDPIRG, a research group, today reported 20 volunteer surveyors checked prices at 27 food chain stores over the weekend. The report showed Sav-Mor had cut prices the most.

"I do not expect milk prices to drop much more," Michael J. Jeffries, co-director of MIDPIRG, said, "because state law prohibits retailers from selling milk below cost."

Last year, MIDPIRG (Midcity Public Interest Research Group) reported a half gallon of homogenized milk was selling for $1.89. The $1.89 was the minimum previously allowed by the state.

Over the weekend, MIDPIRG found the major chains had cut milk prices $.08 to $1.81 per half gallon, except Sav-Mor where the price was $1.80 per half gallon. MIDPIRG reported that independent food stores were charging anywhere from $1.83 to $1.85 per half gallon of milk.

1-I

(MIDCITY)—It is estimated that more than 38,000 local students have not been vaccinated for rubeola measles despite an intensive immunization program last week by the Midcity Unified School District and the Midcity Health Department, said Donna W. Miller, dir. of MUSD nursing services.

Over 50% (40,090) of the district's students were vaccinated last week, but 38,020 still must be immunized, Miller reported.

"From now on, we will refer students to the health department or their private physicians for their shots," Miller announced.

There is plenty of the rubeola measles vaccine available, according to Dr. Donald V. Shay, chief of acute communicable disease control for the Midcity Health Department.

"We need to get all students vaccinated," Shay said, "because we might have an epidemic of 10-day rubeola measles this year if we don't."

1-J

(TAMPA, Fla.)—The pilot and co-pilot of the National Airlines DC-9 that crashed here yesterday, killing 43 passengers, have refused to take blood alcohol tests, a spokesman for the National Transportation Safety Board, said today.

Board public affairs director Lowell F. Frazier said federal investigators requested the blood test from pilot Gary V. Merced, 54, and co-pilot Janice M. Danielson, 41, as well as a standard urinalysis. But they were only able to get urine samples from the two.

The urinalysis is required under federal laws, but the blood test is optional.

No official word yet from the NTSB about the cause of the crash.

1-K

(MIDCITY)—A motorcyclist died and a Midcity police officer was injured early today in back-to-back accidents on Interstate 15 near downtown. Dead at the scene was Martin P. O'Brien, 33, 2764 W. Clearview Dr. O'Brien was traveling south on the interstate about 2:55 a.m. when he lost control of his motorcycle, hit the center divider and was thrown to the pavement, according to a Midcity Police Department report.

After Midcity Police Officer Raul J. Torres, 27, stopped at the scene to assist the motorcyclist, both he and O'Brien were struck by a car just south of the Makapu St. overpass, the MPD reported. Officials stated it was uncertain if O'Brien was killed from falling off his motorcycle or from being hit by the car.

Torres is listed in stable condition at Kaiser Hospital. The driver of the car was identified as Brenda L. Chu, 21, 8428 Carnation Ave. She was arrested on charges of felony drunken driving and reckless driving, MPD officials said.

1-L

(AUSTIN, Tex.)—The Texas Senate, spurred by the case of a Houston woman ticketed for using a men's restroom at a crowded concert hall, today adopted a "potty parity" bill designed to relieve long lines at women's public lavatories.

The bill would require large sports and entertainment facilities built or renovated from the first of the year on to have twice as many women's restrooms as men's restrooms.

The Governor of Texas, Maria E. Castro, has promised to sign the bill next week. She said she has been the victim of long lines at women's restrooms for years and it was time stadium officials and event promoters showed more consideration for women.

● RADIO NEWSCAST 2

2-A

(MIDCITY)—An early morning fire gutted the Midcity Boy's and Girl's Club, 1797 Johnson Ave., causing damage estimated at up to $475,000, according to fire officials.

Officials said they suspect arson and are investigating the 2:10 a.m. blaze that completely destroyed the Boy's and Girl's Club building and a great deal of new gymnastics equipment that had arrived at the club just two days before.

The fire appeared to have started in the upper floor office area, according to Fire Capt. Robert C. Tinker.

"When we pulled up, flames were through the office roof and it was so hot you could hardly get inside," Tinker said. "Heavy roof tiles were falling in chunks. It was so hot it melted the Coke machine."

No injuries were reported.

Three engine companies and 17 firefighters fought the fire for more than five hours.

"It's a total loss," said Eugene F. Magee, club manager. "I don't know what our 257 members are going to do now that the building is destroyed. I guess we'll have to look for another building. I don't know where we're going to get the money, though."

2-B

(MIDCITY)—A family argument involving several persons was blamed for the shooting death last night of Raymond P. Rayburn, 38, 2020 Norton Ave., shortly after 11:00 p.m., according to Midcity Police.

Arrested and charged with murder was William W. Taite, 62, 4581 Pixley Dr., the victim's father-in-law.

Witnesses reported that Taite, Taite's son, Timothy L. Taite, 29, and Rayburn began arguing over family financial matters. Rayburn reportedly pushed the elder Taite to the floor of the Ox Tail Bar, 1675 Main St., after a brief scuffle. The elder Taite left the bar, but returned a few minutes later waving a gun.

The elder Taite walked over to Rayburn, who was sitting with his wife, Catherine M. Rayburn, 35, witnesses reported. After uttering a number of obscenities, the elder Taite fired two shots into Rayburn's chest, witnesses added.

Rayburn died at the scene, according to the Midcity County Coroner's Department.

2-C

(LOS ANGELES)—FedMart Corp., an ailing chain of discount food and general merchandise stores in the Southwest, announced today that it will permanently close all of its stores over the next several months, throwing more than 10,000 company employees out of work.

The announcement was made in a letter to workers at FedMart's 56 stores by Walter J. Heen, pres. of the Los Angeles-based company.

"Under current economic and labor conditions, it was the only choice possible," Heen said in the letter.

The recession, rising unemployment, rising interest rates and high unionized employee wages have been particularly hard on discount retailers, such as FedMart, which generally depend on less-affluent customers, said Dr. Jorge T. Macias, prof. of economics at the University of Southern California.

Most of FedMart's 56 stores are in Southern California. The company also has stores in Arizona, Nevada and New Mexico.

2-D

(WASHINGTON, D.C.)—The nation's steel producers—US Steel, Bethlehem Steel, Inland Steel, and Wheeling-Pittsburgh Steel—announced late last night that they have decided to delay a 5.5% price increase that was scheduled to take effect the first day of next month.

No reason for the delay was announced.

Industry sources believe competition from foreign steel producers forced the delay, but they expect some increase in prices will surely come sometime within the next year. They refused to speculate on a specific date or specific amount for the projected increase, however.

2-E

(MIDCITY)—The vice-president of the Ohio College of Technology (OCT) has been named the new president of West Midcity Community College, filling the leadership position there which has been open for 18 months.

The appointment of Dr. H. H. "Buck" Jones, who had served at OCT for 6 years, was announced today at an open meeting of WMCC faculty, staff, administrators and students, a college spokesperson said.

Jones, 45, will assume his new duties next month at the 5-year-old private college. His appointment ended a search of more than one year for a president to succeed Dr. William B. Bleyer, 63, who resigned 18 months ago for health reasons.

Jones earned his Ph.D. in economics at Purdue University in Indiana.

2-F

(MIAMI, Fla.)—Daniel V. and Elena L. Zimmer have been married three times—to each other—in four months, but the couple still isn't together. It seems government red tape is keeping the bride at her home in Lima, Peru, and forcing the bridegroom to resume the life of a bachelor here.

"Sure, I miss Elena," Zimmer said. "Hearing her voice on the phone is okay, but it's not like being married, if you know what I mean. We love each other and all we want is to be together."

Zimmer, a grocery clerk, and Elena were first married aboard the "Blissful Voyage," a Miami-based ocean liner, but Zimmer said his parents wanted a church wedding, so the couple married again.

On the honeymoon, Elena decided she wanted to be married in Lima so her family could attend. Zimmer, 33, agreed, but after a large church wedding and reception, which was attended by several high-ranking Peruvian governmental officials, the former Elena Villa, 21, found that being the wife of an American citizen did not help solve a snafu in getting U.S. immigration officials to grant her a visa.

James G. O'Keefe, district director of the U.S. Immigration office here, said he did not know what was causing the delay.

"I feel for them, I really do," O'Keefe said, "so I hope we can work things out and they can be together."

2-G

(MIDCITY)—Twenty-six persons, most of them students from a high school here, were injured this morning when a large truck driven by a Midcity man collided with the rear of a school bus en route to an outing at the Midcity Zoo, the Midcity Police reported.

Officers said the accident occurred at 7:55 a.m. on Interstate 5 about three miles north of the zoo when a semi-trailer truck struck the rear of the bus from Western High School.

The bus, driven by Alonzo J. Castro, 39, carried 56 students and 6 chaperones. The truck was driven by Mark F. Nelson, 27, 858 N. Mound St.

Both drivers were injured in the collision, but the injuries were not serious. The drivers and the other slightly injured students and chaperones were treated at Midcity Community Hospital and released.

Nelson was cited for following another vehicle at an unsafe distance.

2-H

<u>NEWS RELEASE</u>

TO: Midcity News Media
FROM: Midcity District Attorney's Office

FOR IMMEDIATE RELEASE

District Attorney Edward F. Whittler has proposed that a task force be formed to review local election ordinances and to suggest amendments if necessary.

In a letter to the Board of Supervisors, Whittler said he thought an investigation was necessary in light of last week's indictments of two former officials of a local construction company for violating campaign ordinances by allegedly making corporate contributions to the campaign committee of Supervisor Linda M. Anderson.

Whittler suggested the task force include representatives of the Board of Supervisors, district attorney, registrar of voters, city clerk, Common Cause, and the League of Women Voters.

Among the areas Whittler suggested be reviewed are the effectiveness and level of campaign contribution limitations, the effectiveness of prohibitions against organization contributions, and the advisability of imposing separate controls on an officeholder's off-year political funds.

"We've got to clean up some of the loose ends and loopholes or we're in for some real problems," Whittler said. "I think now is a good time to do it."

2-I

NEWS RELEASE

TO: Midcity News Media
FROM: Midcity Office of Public Affairs
SUBJECT: Midcity Stadium Noise Abatement

                                        FOR IMMEDIATE RELEASE

    Paul M. Gade, Midcity Noise Abatement Officer, will recommend that the Midcity Board of Supervisors invest in a $19,875 device that would automatically govern the amplification of music played at Midcity Stadium so as to conform with the city's noise control law.

    Gade calls the device a novel way to muffle the sound level of rock concerts at the stadium.

    "It's not going to suddenly shut off the sound, though," said Gade.

    Gade plans to recommend the purchase and installation of the device when he appears before the board's Public Facilities and Recreation Committee next Tuesday night.

    Rock groups would pay a small fee for the use of the device.

    "We don't want to ruin rock concerts for the people who enjoy them," said Gade. "We just want to tone down the noise a bit and protect the rights of the non-rock lovers."

    Gade said his office received more than 50 complaints from Midcity Stadium neighbors after the recent concert by the group "Heavy Metal." The group used 36 amplifiers and attained a decibel level well above that permitted in the city's noise regulations, stated Gade.

    Gade believes monitoring the power supply of rock musicians to regulate the output of decibels is the only way to save the ears and windows of persons living near the stadium.

    Several communities in other states use the device, known as the "Noise Capper," stated Gade.

2-J

(MIDCITY)—Sarah Jane Tippler, 18, 1745 Washington Ave., was pronounced dead at the scene of a one-car crash at the corner of Mercer Street and Oak Avenue last night at 11:50 p.m. that also critically injured her passenger, Arnold C. Curran, 19, 3589 Oak Ave. Curran is undergoing treatment at Midcity General Hospital.

Tippler was driving west in the 3300 block of Oak Avenue when she apparently lost control of her car and rammed into a telephone pole, according to Sgt. Marsha D. Whittmer of the Midcity Police Department.

2-K

(MIDCITY)—A legal bid to have a Midcity chain store take down signs labeling certain toys "boys toys" and other toys "girls toys" began this morning before Superior Court Judge Milton R. Thompson. The case is a class action suit against Buy-Rite Drug Stores, Inc.

"The issue is children's mental health," said Gloria C. Sakamoto, attorney for the plaintiffs—seven children and the Women's Equal Rights Legal Defense and Education Foundation.

By putting dolls and cookware in an aisle labeled "girls toys" and play money and tools in an aisle designated "boys toys," Sakamoto alleged that Buy-Rite perpetuates sexual stereotyping, which is unfair.

Sakamoto added that she was particularly angered by Buy-Rite's argument that the designations were justified by the genetic differences between boys and girls.

The attorney for Buy-Rite, John J. Torgerson, said the practice of labeling the toys was a "time-saving device" meant to assist customers.

The hearing on the suit continues tomorrow morning.

2-L

(LOS ANGELES)—A fire destroyed the famed Bonaventure Hotel here this morning. Three elderly residents were killed and 42 persons were injured in the three-alarm blaze.

Firefighters battled the fire for nine hours before controlling it. No other buildings were affected.

"We're not positive about the cause of the fire yet, but it looks as if it probably was started by some faulty wiring in the kitchen area," said Los Angeles Fire Department Capt. Stephen P. Acker.

Damage estimates have been set at $12,000,000.

All the victims died from smoke inhalation. Many of the injured suffered burns as they raced through flames which at times reached as high as 10 feet. More than 350 persons had to be evacuated.

● RADIO NEWSCAST 3

3-A

(MIDCITY)—A local bar was robbed early today by four masked men armed with shotguns and pistols who shot open the safe after the bartender refused to give up the key, police said. The robbers escaped on foot with an undisclosed amount of cash.

The bartender, Stacy P. Gale, 23, 9841 Mercer Ave., was kicked in the stomach when she failed to provide the key to the safe in the back room, police added.

After taking wallets from Gale and the sole customer in the establishment—"Sally's Saloon," 2959 Broadway Ave., downtown—three of the men started to leave the bar, but the fourth returned to the back room.

"I'm going to shoot this sucker open, man," the robber was quoted by Gale as saying.

Police said the robber fired three shots with a handgun in blasting open the safe. After removing the contents from the safe, all four robbers escaped on foot.

Police estimate the robbers got away with more than $5,000, but no official word on the exact amount was immediately available.

The robbery occurred at 1:50 a.m.

3-B

(HONOLULU)—James H. Epperlein, a former mayor of Midcity for three terms in the 1950s and 1960s, died here today after a long illness. He was 83.

Elected as mayor in 1952 for his first term, Epperlein held the position until 1964, when he was defeated by Margaret W. Jenkins, Midcity's first woman mayor.

Epperlein became the chief executive officer of the First Hawaiian Bank of Honolulu in 1965. He retired from that position in 1985.

The Midcity native graduated from Midcity University in 1942. He was a member of the varsity football team and worked on the student newspaper, "The Daily Tiger."

Epperlein is survived by his wife, Constance, four children and 12 grandchildren. Services will be held early next week in Honolulu at the Yamashita Mortuary.

3-C

(Reporter Voicer—KCTI Reporter Nancy Kim)

Public hearings start tomorrow on the city's proposed $812,000,000 budget. Budget is a 4% increase over last year's, but inflation locally has been running at about 6%. Lots of cuts are expected in programs. Hearings will start at 9:00 a.m. at Board of Supervisors chambers, 1700 Burton Ln.

KIM VOICER IN: "We can expect bumpier roads and 'pay-for-play' tennis courts if all the expected budget cuts are made."

KIM VOICER OUT: "Nancy Kim reporting for KCTI Radio news."

KIM TAPE TIME: :30

3-D

(MIDCITY)—A local couple was taken into custody today in connection with the poisoning yesterday of four of the five dogs owned by Mrs. Anna V. Webster, 49, 6392 N. 57th St.

Paul J. Lowe, 33, 6387 Pike Dr., and Barbara B. Lowe, 31, were booked into Midcity County Jail on charges of felony cruelty to animals after the Midcity Humane Society executed a warrant signed by Municipal Court Judge William D. Howatt.

The Lowes, Webster's back neighbors, face four counts each of felony dog poisoning and cruelty to animals, Midcity Humane Society Capt. Michael G. Shirley said today. Some meat laced with strychnine was tossed yesterday into Webster's yard where four Afghan hounds and a poodle were kept. Three of the Afghans and the poodle died.

3E

(MIDCITY)—Midcity Fire Capt. Gary J. Spaulding, 39, pleaded innocent today before Municipal Court Judge Darlene A. Chaney on charges of petty theft, receiving stolen property, and carrying a concealed weapon, a loaded gun.

Craig H. Gunnersley, defense counsel, and Brenda S. Kelly, deputy district attorney, agreed to meet next week to discuss the case against Spaulding before setting a preliminary hearing date.

Spaulding has been free on bond since his arrest last month at a home building site in North Midcity. Police, investigating a prowler call, said they found Spaulding loading his car with several bags of copper pipe taken from the site.

Spaulding was suspended without pay from the Midcity Fire Department pending the outcome of the charges against him.

3-F

<u>**News from Midcity University**</u>

University News Service
800-555-5555

FOR IMMEDIATE RELEASE

MU STUDENTS LIKE THEIR SCHOOL

A recent poll of Midcity University students shows that despite the complaints often heard about the university, the majority give MU high evaluations.

Paul J. Strand, director of the MU Poll, reports that 92% of the students surveyed are satisfied with life in general at the university and 85% are satisfied with the school's academic programs.

Location and quality of education are among the most popular features of the university. More than 22% of the students indicated they continue to attend MU because of its location. More than 27% of the students indicated they continue to attend because of the quality of education MU provides. When asked whether they were satisfied or dissatisfied with the quality of education here, only 18% of the students indicated any dissatisfaction.

Despite high evaluations, the university does have some drawbacks. More than 67% of the students were dissatisfied with registration procedures. Nearly 60% were dissatisfied with the number of parking spaces available for students. Almost 50% of the students felt MU was too overcrowded.

The survey results were based on telephone interviews conducted last month with a scientifically selected sample of 400 students. The margin of error for this survey is approximately plus or minus 5%.

MU plans to conduct similar polls each semester to keep officials abreast of student perspectives and needs.

3-G

(Actuality Available)

Midcity schoolteachers are still on strike. Day 5 for the strike of K-12 teachers.

Official Midcity Unified School District reports indicate a 50% attendance rate by students, but the Midcity Teachers Association says the attendance is much lower—closer to 25%.

No violence yet. Atmosphere is relatively calm and friendly on the picket lines in front of schools and the district offices.

Some strikebreakers, but they, so far, are being treated kindly.

Dist. Supt. Eric A. Otterman reported most of the district's 2,559 teachers remained on strike, but their places have been taken by 1,043 substitute teachers who are each being paid $100 per day.

Otterman said the district is pursuing legal action against the MTA, but he would not elaborate further.

The Midcity Board of Education met in special session last night and upped its 8% salary increase offer to 10%. Teacher officials say they intend to hold out for 15%.

The Board of Education has scheduled another special session tonight at Lincoln High School at 7:00 p.m. in the Roan Cafeteria.

Both teacher officials and district officials say the only thing standing in the way of ending the strike is the money impasse.

The average teacher pay in Midcity is $29,900.

(Actuality with Karley W. Aaron, a 3rd grade teacher who has refused to strike. She was interviewed at her job at Hamilton Elementary School.)

AARON ACTUALITY: (TAPE TIME :15)
"I'm one of the few regular teachers still teaching, because the strike is simply against my own personal principles. My sympathies are completely with my friends and colleagues out on the picket lines. We teachers are overworked and underpaid, but I just cannot bring myself to walk out on my students. They need me."

3-H

(MIDCITY)—Burglars took an estimated $55,000 worth of jewelry late last night from the "Gem of a Store" boutique in Fashion Square, Midcity Police reported.

The thieves bypassed the burglar alarm system by removing a glass panel in a skylight and slipping through the opening in the roof, police said.

The burglary was the fourth at the boutique in the last two months.

Police have no suspects.

3-I

(CHICAGO)—Melinda J. Russell, the so-called "Welfare Queen," who welfare officials report is the biggest welfare chiseler of all time, was sentenced today to 5-10 years in prison.

Miss Russell, alias Linda Russ, Roxanne Lind, Melinda Lindholm, Linda Russe, and others, was convicted last month of theft and perjury.

Prosecutors said the offenses for which she was convicted resulted in her obtaining $197,875.50, but investigators say her schemes, aliases and disguises were so numerous and intricate that it would be impossible to ascertain precisely how much she bilked welfare agencies out of.

An investigation shows she used her many aliases and disguises to obtain at least $397,498.50 for medical assistance, cash assistance and bonus food stamps, said Walter P. Bickman, dir. of the Illinois Public Aid Department.

"Miss Russell is without a doubt the biggest welfare cheat of all time," Bickman pronounced. "She's been living the good life at the expense of the government and of the people who really need assistance. I'm glad we got her. I only wish her sentence was heavier."

Russell, 49, refused to talk with reporters after the sentencing.

3-J

(CAMPO, Calif.)—The ad in the "Campo Courier" read "Chicken, 57¢ a pound."

So, when Brian M. Sayers, 36, opened his Campo General Store, sheriff's deputies were first in line this morning.

The deputies arrested Sayers and Samuel P. Hall, 28, an employee at the store, and charged them with grand larceny.

Deputies alleged the 5,000 pounds of chicken at Sayer's store came from the 65-crate shipment of chicken that was stolen from the Campo Poultry Works three days ago. Deputies became suspicious, they said, when chicken worth at least $1.89 a pound was advertised for just 57¢.

Campo is a small farming town of about 3,000 persons. It is 60 miles northeast of San Diego.

3-K

(MIDCITY)—A 9-year-old Midcity boy died here today after he fell out of the back of a pickup truck being driven by his father, police reported.

Another young boy died in a separate accident this morning, but his name has not been released pending notification of next of kin.

In the truck accident, Dennis Dean Tappen, Jr., 2541 Bisbee Ave., fell out of the pickup at 7:45 a.m. as it was making a turn from Norwood St. to Roxanne Dr. He was taken to Midcity General Hospital, but died a short time later, police said.

In the other accident, a 7-year-old boy was killed when he was struck by a car. The boy was crossing in the middle of Bevers St. when he was struck by a car driven by Marilyn Y. Kepperman, 54, 6196 Pearl Ave. Kepperman was not cited. The accident occurred at 7:25 a.m.

The boy was taken to Midcity Memorial Hospital but was pronounced dead en route.

3-L

(Actuality Available)

(CINCINNATI)—An explosion blamed on coal dust ripped apart part of a brick factory here today, injuring 9 employees.

The explosion set off a fire that roared through a building which was more than 100 yards long, but the fire was brought under control quickly.

A spokesperson for the Cincinnati Fire Department said one building in the Meadows and Heighton Co. factory collapsed after the explosion at 8:15 a.m.

The 9 injured workers were taken to Cincinnati General Hospital. Two were listed in critical condition, two in serious condition and five in fair condition.

Edward K. Kaiser, a spokesperson for the company, estimated the damage at more than $2,500,000.

(Actuality with Nelson C. Bentley, chief, Cincinnati Fire Department)

BENTLEY ACTUALITY (TAPE TIME :10)
"It looks as if the fire started when some coal dust was ignited by one of the furnaces in the plant. We got everybody out, though. There were 16 employees in the plant when the explosion occurred and we've accounted for all 16. It's a real mess, though. That's for sure."

● RADIO NEWSCAST 4

4-A

(MILWAUKEE)—Nurse Wilma E. Huston was fed up with people sneaking sips from her bottled water at Tripler Memorial Hospital here. So, police said, she got even.

Huston, 34, of Milwaukee, is charged with willfully poisoning another nurse by dumping a clear solution used to preserve tissue samples into a bottle of water bearing her name and placing it in a refrigerator shared by nurses.

The Milwaukee County District Attorney's Office filed charges against Huston today. A Tripler Memorial Hospital spokesperson said Huston has been fired.

According to police, Huston was annoyed that people kept drinking the bottled water that she purchased and brought for her own use. So, three days ago, she told fellow surgery nurse Ruth D. Bohanen, 46, that she was going to put formalin, a clear chemical used in the operating room, in her water "to teach a lesson" to the water thief. Bohanen said she laughed off the threat as a joke.

But yesterday, Bohanen, also of Milwaukee, took a sip from a water bottle with Huston's name on it and soon felt a burning in her throat. She was admitted to the hospital and treated for poisoning. Her symptoms included nausea, vomiting and throat irritation. She is expected to be released from the hospital tomorrow.

Huston admitted dumping the formalin into the water bottle.

"I feel a little guilty about it," Huston said, "but people shouldn't take things that belong to somebody else. Seems to me you get what you get when you steal from somebody."

4-B

(Actuality Available)

(MIDCITY)—Nice guys might not finish last all the time, but they can get stiffed in a fake wedding ring scam. Just ask James R. Smith.

Smith, 45, according to the Midcity Police, got a lesson on the consequences of gullibility yesterday when a pregnant woman came into his Chevron station on Lake Mumford Blvd. near Naranca Rd. and asked for the key to the restroom. Right after she went in, a man called the gas station and said he might have left his $5,000 wedding ring in the restroom and told Smith he'd pay a $1,000 reward to whoever found it.

While the man was still on the phone, the woman returned the key and said she had found a valuable-looking ring in the restroom. The caller said he was elated and promised to give Smith and the woman $500 each as soon as he got back to the station in about 45 minutes.

The woman said she couldn't wait and asked Smith to give her $500 out of the register and then he could keep the entire $1,000 when the man showed up to claim the ring. Smith agreed. The man never showed.

Last week, according to police, a similar attempt at what is called theft by deception was tried at another gas station in town, but the attendant didn't fall for the scam.

SMITH ACTUALITY (TAPE TIME :10)
"I told my boss what happened and he said I could pay him back out of my paycheck a little each month. I feel like such a fool. She seemed so nice. She was pregnant and everything."

4-C

(SEATTLE)—A pregnant woman said her condition gave her the right to drive in a freeway lane requiring at least two people per car, but a judge did not agree with her. Seattle Municipal Court Judge Deborah H. Sing found Mary Ellen Keppler, of Snohomish, Wash., guilty of violating the freeway carpool ordinance and fined her $47. Keppler, who was stopped for driving alone in the HOV (high-occupancy-vehicle) lane, told the judge that she did not think she was doing anything wrong.

"I am a nurse and every nurse I know considers a fetus a person, so I felt I had two persons in my car," she testified.

Judge Sing told Keppler that the guilty verdict was not based on the broader issues of when a fetus is considered a person. It was, Sing said, limited to the question of whether legislators intended for a fetus to be considered a passenger when it came to determining how many persons were in a car traveling in the HOV lane.

"I believe legislators had in mind two separated, distinct, air-breathing, living human beings when they drafted the legislation," Sing pronounced.

4-D

(MIDCITY)—For the second time in less than a year, the district attorney has filed charges against Food King Grocery Co. for overcharging, it was announced today.

The charges, filed against the company and supervisors from 8 of its stores, cite repeated discrepancies between prices posted on the stores' shelves and what was programmed into the checkout scanners, said Dist. Atty. Edward F. Whittler.

Most of the violations occurred, Whittler said, when clerks failed to remove sale tags once the discounts had ended.

Eight months ago, Food King paid $15,500 in fines related to similar charges. This time, fines could run as high as $31,000 if all the current charges are upheld.

Attorneys for Food King said they will have to review all of the particulars related to the charges before they will have a response.

Food King is the second largest supermarket chain in Midcity with 12 local stores. Food Basket is the largest local supermarket chain with 17 stores.

4-E

(MIDCITY)—Helium balloons, possibly released from someone's party, may have contributed to the crash of a light plane that killed the pilot, according to a federal report released today.

Last month, Adam R. Dickerson, 57, 632 Caldecott Ave., died in the crash near Gilligan's Field, a rural airport in East Midcity. His Piper PA-30 Twin Comanche slammed into a hillside at about 120 mph.

A witness, who was on horseback near the crash site, reported she heard a popping sound and saw what appeared to be confetti falling as the plane nosedived into the hillside, according to a National Transportation Safety Board report.

The NTSB report surmised that the pilot was probably flying too low, hit the free-floating balloons and lost control of his plane.

4-F

(WASHINGTON)—More than 25% of the girls who drop out of high school cite pregnancy as the reason—and nearly 8% of the boys who drop out say it is because they have become parents.

But the most common reason for dropping out of high school is a simple dislike for school, the Department of Education reported today.

In its annual dropout report, the department said 381,000 high school students aged 13-18 quit school last year. That translates to approximately 11% of the total number of 13-to-18-year-olds who should be attending school.

About 52% of the total sample—61% of the boys and 45% of the girls—reported they were either bored by school, tired of going to school, not interested in school or simply did not like school.

Other popular reasons for dropping out of school were a need to work, moving and family hardships including deaths, divorces and illnesses.

4-G

(LONDON)—Medical students should be taught acting so they can give patients better emotional support, according to two Canadian doctors.

Writing in the British medical journal *The Lancet*, which was published today, David P. Conway and Edmund G. Blinn in their article entitled "Doctors as Actors: The Time Has Come for a Required Course" said, "We think doctors must be actors and they must become much better actors than they are now."

Dr. Blinn, a specialist who often treats people with chronic pain, believes it is essential for doctors to convey messages of concern and encouragement to patients, their families and their friends.

Dr. Conway and Dr. Blinn wrote that medical training should include an acting curriculum focusing on conveying "appropriate and beneficial responses to the emotional needs of patients, family and friends."

The doctors believe that doctors should be much more sensitive to what have heretofore been considered "non-medical attributes" of patient care.

"Sometimes doctors are called upon to 'fake it' a bit," Dr. Conway said in an interview. "Acting lessons should be a required course of study for all doctors so they'll be better equipped to treat the whole patient."

4-H

(ARTESIA, N.M.)—Somehow the new name fits.

A dog, who's name used to be Brownie is now called Zombie. The reason why is something right out of an Ed Wood Jr. Grade B movie.

Three days ago, Brenda C. Frazier, 41, of Artesia, ran over her dog, Brownie.

"He looked dead," Frazier said. "He wasn't breathing or moving."

She asked the rest of her family to examine Brownie and all but one family member agreed with her. Frazier's 5-year-old son, Brandon, refused to believe his dog was dead.

"Brownie not dead," the boy said.

Since the family consensus was that Brownie was in fact dead, the family buried him in a field near their house. But Brownie, like little Brandon, didn't believe he was dead, either.

Yesterday, when the family returned from a trip to Carlsbad, 30 miles away, a dirt-covered Brownie was on the porch.

"He was cold and he wasn't breathing too good," Mrs. Frazier said. "It freaked me out. He looked bad."

The mixed-breed dog lost an eye and broke his right shoulder in the accident.

"He was no ghost, though," veterinarian Michael S. Winston said. "He obviously wasn't dead. He was probably just in a coma."

The dog has responded well to treatment and now has a new name: Zombie, after the returned-from-the-dead characters in horror movies.

The Fraziers say they are not sure if Brownie-Zombie dug himself out of his shallow grave or if he was dug out by the family's other three dogs.

"We're just glad he's alive," Mrs. Frazier said.

4-I

(MIDCITY)—A construction worker was killed this morning in an accident at a local doughnut shop.

The man was working alone with a motorized saw on the roof the Donut Hut at 589 N. Madison Ave. when the saw apparently kicked back and cut him in the groin, severing an artery, according to Midcity Police.

Officers arrived at the Donut Hut at 8:43 a.m. and the man was pronounced dead shortly after they arrived.

"He bled to death within 8 minutes," said Maria Y. Lopez, dep. coroner.

The man's name is being withheld pending notification of next of kin.

4-J

(NAGOYA, Japan)—A Taiwanese jet apparently trying to abort a landing, crashed, exploded and burned beside an airport runway last night, killing 261 persons. Ten persons survived.

The crash of the China Airlines A300-600R Airbus was Japan's second worst aviation disaster.

Minutes before the crash, pilot Wang Lo-chi radioed that he would have to try another landing attempt, because he did not like his first attempt.

A survivor, Sylvanie Detonio of the Philippines, was quoted by Fuji TV as saying passengers received no warning that the plane was in trouble.

Flight 140 carried 256 passengers and a crew of 15 bound from Taipei, Taiwan to Nagoya. Most of the passengers were from Japan or Taiwan.

The A300-600R, a twin-engine wide-body jet, has not been involved in a crash before; however, other A300 models have been involved in 6 accidents.

Japan's worst aviation disaster—the worst single-plane accident in history anywhere—occurred on Aug. 12, 1985, when a Japan Airlines Boeing 747 crashed into a mountain on a domestic flight, killing 520 people.

4-K

(Reporter Voicer—KCTI Reporter Connie Cameron)

Is it a dog or is it a wolf? That's the question the Board of Supervisors will have to address at its next meeting. Bandit is a 5-year-old wolf hybrid who, technically, is a lawbreaker. His owners say Bandit is really more dog than wolf. He likes to play with kids and is really kind of shy. Nevertheless, his owners are not only fighting to keep their pet, they're fighting for the animal's life.

Last week, a neighbor complained to city authorities that she thought a wolf was being kept in the neighborhood. Keeping a wild animal within the city limits is against the law and a wolf is considered a wild animal. Because of the complaint, Bandit may have to find a new home or he may even have to be put to sleep.

If the Board of Supervisors decides Bandit is indeed a wolf, his owners will have 30 days to dispose of the animal. If Bandit is declared a dog, he can remain within the city limits.

Reporter Connie Cameron has talked with Bandit's owners, city officials and animal rights organizations.

CAMERON VOICER IN: "Bill and Kathleen Smith say their Bandit is a lot more dog than wolf."

CAMERON VOICER OUT: "From West Midcity, I'm Connie Cameron for KCTI Radio news."

CAMERON TAPE TIME: :36

4-L

(Actuality Available)

(EDISON, N.J.)—A natural gas pipeline exploded early today creating an inferno that engulfed six apartment buildings, but left just one person dead and 59 persons injured in what a local official called "a miracle." The 4:00 a.m. blast created a 60-foot-wide crater, leveling the buildings.

"When you tour the site," New Jersey Gov. Christie Whitman told a news conference at the scene, "you see what ground zero after a nuclear blast would be like."

The explosion sent flames 300 feet into the air, lighting up the sky. Witnesses in New York City, 25 miles away, said they saw the flames.

Whitman said the low casualty total was probably due to a 10-minute gap between the initial explosion and the fire that followed. The gap gave shaken residents time to evacuate.

The steel pipeline, which stretches from Texas to New Jersey, is 36-inches wide. Officials said they could not explain how the pipeline, which is buried 7-feet under ground, ruptured and burst into flames.

(Actuality from George Spadoro, mayor of Edison, N.J.)

SPADORO ACTUALITY (TAPE TIME :08)

"We sent an especially trained dog through the destroyed buildings twice and the dog found no human remains. It's definitely a miracle. We've got to get busy now and find housing for those people who've lost their homes."

- ## TV READER 1

Rewrite the following in correct KCTI news style. (TRT :15)

(SAN FRANCISCO)—Anthony S. Kennedy, 78, who was wounded in the invasion of Normandy, June 14, 1944, received his Purple Heart award yesterday. The citation came in the mail postmarked last week, without any explanation of why it was late.

    Kennedy is a retired California Department of Motor Vehicles employee. He lives here.

    A spokesperson for the U.S. Department of Defense claimed officials were looking into the matter.

    A spokesperson for the U.S. Postal Service explained that occasionally letters are temporarily lost or misplaced, but a delay of more than 50 years is quite unusual.

- ## TV READER 2

Using correct KCTI news style, write a television news story from the following information. (TRT :15)

Priscilla Ann Rivers, 38, was killed this morning when she was struck by two cars as she walked on Dole St. near Midcity Community College.

Accident occurred at 9:35 a.m.

Rivers was pronounced dead at the scene of the accident.

Rivers was hit by a car driven by Gary J. Johnson, 20, 1836 May Way, according to police. The impact of the collision threw Rivers into the path of a car going in the opposite direction. The second car was driven by Alice B. Thomas, 54, 7529 Baxter Dr. Neither driver was cited. Rivers was not in a crosswalk when she was hit by Johnson's car.

Death was number 105 in Midcity's traffic toll this year.

● TV READER 3

Rewrite the following in correct KCTI news style. (TRT :30)

News from Midcity University

University News Service
800 555-5555

FOR IMMEDIATE RELEASE

SPORTS TERMINATED AT MIDCITY UNIVERSITY

Men's and women's swimming will continue as intercollegiate sports at Midcity University, but women's field hockey, men's and women's badminton, and men's water polo will be terminated effective immediately, it was announced today by Midcity University President Philip A. Longley.

The move was made in order to utilize limited resources more effectively and provide a better balance to men's and women's programs, Longley added.

The action by Longley came after studying a proposal from the school's Department of Athletics via Melissa J. Rodriguez, Director of Athletics, which called for the termination of women's field hockey, men's and women's swimming, men's water polo and men's and women's badminton.

The approved changes will allow for a modest strengthening of support for volleyball, basketball, gymnastics, and tennis—all major women's sports programs—and for streamlining the women's athletic program, Longley noted.

"Our purpose," Longley remarked, "is to use our resources more effectively. Our ambitions have outstripped our means, though. If we are to achieve the quality of excellence we seek in our athletic programs, we must limit the number of programs we support."

● TV READER 4

Rewrite the following in correct KCTI news style. (TRT :20)

(MIDCITY)—Ruby M. Tybo had no problem disputing hospital charges for labor and delivery room services. She's 89, and the youngest of her three children is nearly 60.

"I just nearly flipped my lid," Tybo said of the $993 insurance statement she received yesterday from Midcity Memorial Hospital.

The new-baby charges were included with a statement on fees for physical therapy she completed last month.

A hospital official said the fee was a computer error that resulted from a computer coding mistake that slipped by unnoticed.

"We're extremely sorry for any inconvenience our error may have caused Mrs. Tybo," Maria P. Longfeather said, "but it's kind of funny when you think about it, isn't it?"

Medicare did not catch the mistaken computer code, either. It paid the bill from Midcity Memorial Hospital without questioning the listed fees.

● **TV READER 5**

Rewrite the following in correct KCTI news style. (TRT :20)

(WASHINGTON, D.C.)—Next to traffic accidents, gunfire is the most common cause of death for Americans aged 15 to 19 and is rising every year, the government says.

For blacks in that age range, it is the most frequent cause of death.

A study released today by the National Center for Health Statistics said that the gun is the most favored weapon, by a wide margin, for teen-age murder and that the number of young black males killed by gunfire is increasing at a rapid rate in the nation's major metropolitan counties.

The study was published by the *Journal of the American Medical Association*. The lead author of the study, Dr. Lois F. Atwater, said firearm homicide rates rose 10% to 14% in the 1980s, and by 23% to 35% so far in the 1990s.

While the number of firearm homicides increased, homicides with other weapons and deaths from auto accidents actually declined.

Researchers reported the reasons for the increase in firearm homicides included "crack cocaine, changes in the types and lethality of firearms, urban poverty and a myriad of sociological factors."

For the 20 years covered by the study, for white teen-age males, the firearm homicide rate was 16.5 per 100,000. For black teen-age males, the firearm homicide rate was 84.3 per 100,000.

● TV FULL-SCREEN GRAPHICS 1

Rewrite the following in correct KCTI news style. (TRT :20)

(HONOLULU)—Computer expert Douglas M. Caldwell, 31, was arrested here this morning. Caldwell is accused of stealing $15,200,000 from the Bank of Hawaii. Bank officials say someone used a very complicated computer program to divert the money from various accounts into a numbered Swiss bank account.

Caldwell worked for the Bank of Hawaii for five years before he resigned last month. His resignation came one week before the computer transfer of funds was discovered.

Caldwell was arrested this morning at Honolulu International Airport. He was returning from a trip to Los Angeles. He serves as a computer consultant for several small businesses in Los Angeles and San Francisco.

Caldwell has purchased three expensive new cars in the last two weeks despite earning about $40,000 per year with the Bank of Hawaii.

Caldwell will be arraigned tomorrow before Circuit Court Judge Roscoe H. Kalakaua.

Banking experts described the fraud scheme as the largest employee-related theft in the history of banking in the United States.

PICTURE: Caldwell, in handcuffs, being led by police through airport.

● TV FULL-SCREEN GRAPHICS 2

Rewrite the following in correct KCTI news style. (TRT :20)

(SEATTLE)—A bank robber here got more than he bargained for this morning. Paul B. Canfield, 46, robbed the Northwest Federal Savings Bank in downtown Seattle of $57,000.

Canfield got out of the bank with the money without much trouble, after he stuffed the money into pockets in his pants and coat and made his escape on foot, police claim.

Canfield ran into a nearby department store, but there his luck ran out. While in the store, his pants and coat exploded in a cloud of billowing red smoke. It seems a teller, who gave Canfield the money, also gave him explosive money packets containing tear gas and red dye.

As startled bystanders looked on, the suspect dashed into a restroom with smoke gushing from the pockets of his slacks and coat.

Store security personnel detained Canfield until Seattle police officers arrived and arrested Canfield. He was charged with robbery. He was not injured.

PICTURE: Canfield waving arms to dispel smoke. People staring at him.

- ## TV FULL-SCREEN GRAPHICS 3

Write a TV news story in correct KCTI news style from the following information. (TRT :20)

Big earthquake in Southern California this afternoon. No deaths or injuries reported so far. Plenty of property damage, however. Officials at the California Civil Defense Department estimate the damage at $12,000,000. Mostly collapsed ceilings and cracks in walls and pillars.

Earthquake experts at the University of California-San Diego have indicated the epicenter of the quake was about 6 miles east of Santee, California. Santee is a suburb of San Diego, about 10 miles northeast of San Diego. They expect aftershocks throughout the night tonight and all day tomorrow.

Quake measured 5.7 on the Richter Scale. The quake hit at 2:38 p.m. California time. Quake was felt in Los Angeles, San Diego and surrounding cities.

PICTURE: Map showing Santee, San Diego, Los Angeles and Palm Springs. Earthquake epicenter location marked with a large "X" in bright red.

- ## TV FULL-SCREEN GRAPHICS 4

Write a TV news story in correct KCTI news style from the following information. (TRT :20)

Scholastic Assessment Test (SAT) results are in. Midcity students scored a combined 906 on the test of verbal and math skills, down one point from last year. Verbal scores rose one point to 422, but math scores dropped two points to 484. Nationwide averages were 423 verbal, down one point from last year, and 479 math, down two points from last year.

Midcity students have scored higher than the national averages for the past 12 consecutive years, according the Midcity Unified School District officials. This year a record number of Midcity students, 4,296, took the SAT, an increase of 459 over last year.

Each year, the New York-based College Board administers the test to help determine college eligibility. The test measures performance on a scale of 200 to 800 in verbal skills and math skills.

PICTURE: Bar graph of Midcity scores compared to national averages. Midcity scores in bright red and national scores in light blue.

● TV VOICE OVER 1

Write a TV voice over in correct KCTI news style from the following information. Include an on-camera introduction and tail. (TRT :40)

Fire at a warehouse in downtown Midcity. Warehouse owned by Fast-Gro Co., a fertilizer manufacturing company. No fertilizer in building, just a bunch of machinery for packaging it. It was outdated equipment that was just being stored.

Twenty-five firefighters on the scene most of the time. Fire started about 12:00 p.m. and lasted until 3:00 p.m. No injuries. Damage estimate is $485,000. Building was completely destroyed. Clean-up operations lasted until 4:00 p.m. The 2-story warehouse was built in 1937.

Fire Capt. John A. Luter said the fire was caused by an electrical short. The short ignited some gasoline that had spilled on the floor. Luter provided the damage estimate, too.

A warehouse for Tire Town, a local automobile tire store chain, was in danger for a time. The warehouse is next door to the Fast-Gro building. Some tires were rolled out, but when the all-clear was given, workers started rolling the tires back in.

SHOT LIST:

1. Cover shot—flames, firefighters, fire trucks		:06
2. Medium shot—Luter		:04
3. Medium shot—firefighter spraying water		:04
4. Medium shot—flames on building		:04
5. Close-up shot—fire truck		:04
6. Medium shot—workers rolling tires		:06
7. Cover shot—clean up and more tire rolling		:05
	TOTAL	:33

• TV VOICE OVER 2

Write a TV voice over in correct KCTI news style from the following information. Include an on-camera introduction and tail. (TRT :40)

INFORMATION FROM MIDCITY POLICE OFFICERS AT SCENE:

2-car traffic accident at the corner of 54th St. and Western Blvd. Three local persons involved. Driver of one car died at scene. Glen D. Peterson. A passenger in Peterson's car, Anita R. Swann, was not injured.

Driver of the 2nd car, Henry W. Coleman, was not injured. He was arrested and charged with manslaughter. Witnesses reported Coleman ran a stop sign and smashed into the driver's side of Peterson's car.

INFORMATION FROM MARIA Y. LOPEZ, DEP. CORONER:

Peterson died from multiple head injuries caused when his head hit the door on the driver's side. He was not wearing a seat belt.

INFORMATION FROM KCTI PHOTOJOURNALIST EVE BAYANI VANCE:

Coleman was frisked by police. During the incident he kept saying, " I didn't see the stop sign. I didn't see it. It was hidden by a tree branch. I swear I didn't see it."

INFORMATION FROM DAVID M. COHEN, MIDCITY POLICE SPOKESPERSON:

Accident occurred at 7:45 a.m. today. Traffic death #106 in Midcity this year. Coleman booked on felony manslaughter charges. He was taken to Midcity County Jail. Bail set at $50,000.

AGES: Peterson, 29; Swann, 24; Coleman, 44.

ADDRESSES: Peterson, 4523 Niagara Ave.; Swann, 510 State St.; Coleman, 831 Hamilton Dr. #4.

SHOT LIST:
1. Cover shot—cars, police, people	:04
2. Medium shot—covered body	:06
3. Close-up shot—Swann crying	:04
4. Medium shot—police questioning Coleman	:06
5. Medium shot—stop sign and tree branch	:06
6. Cover shot—cars, police, people	:07
TOTAL	:33

● TV VOICE OVER 3

Write a TV voice over in correct KCTI news style from the following information. Include an on-camera introduction and tail. (TRT :40)

News from Midcity University

University News Service
800 555-5555

FOR IMMEDIATE RELEASE

WINDMILLS ARE "IN" AT MIDCITY UNIVERSITY

Students interested in wind power have come to Midcity University from all over the state to learn more about windmills. They are taking part in a special MU Extension Services course, "Windmill Technology."

The course, which will run two weeks, is the first of its kind offered in the United States. It started today and consists of 40 hours of lectures and field experience per week. Twenty-five students are taking the course. They were selected from approximately 175 who applied.

The course is designed to fill the needs of rural communities where qualified windmill technicians are practically nonexistent. Subject material will include history, design, maintenance, and installation of wind-powered machinery for pumping water and generating electricity.

The instructor for the course, Roger S. Litton, has been in the windmill business for 35 years.

"The increasing cost of electricity has really increased the interest in windmills," Litton said. "I look at the course as the university's contribution to the country's energy-saving program."

The United Nations has even sent an observer to monitor the course to see if it might be used to train technicians for third world countries. The observer is from Brazil.

Tuition for the course is $500. Additional courses are planned in future semesters and reservations are already coming in.

For more information, contact the Midcity University News Service.

SHOT LIST:

1. Cover shot—students, instructor, building site	:04
2. Close-up shot—student examining a blueprint	:04
3. Medium shot—windmill blades on ground	:04
4. Medium shot—Litton pointing	:06
5. Medium shot—students working	:04
6. Medium shot—U.N. observer taking notes	:06
7. Cover shot—students, instructor, windmill blades	:05
TOTAL	:33

• TV VOICE OVER 4

Write a TV voice over in correct KCTI news style from the following information. Include an on-camera introduction and tail. (TRT :40)

Plane crash in West Midcity this morning. Plane owned by KMOR Radio. Not much left of plane. Estimated value = $303,000. It was a Cessna 1089. Plane was approximately 3 years old. It was a 4-passenger model. Plane used in the station's "Traffic Watch" reports.

Pilot was Joe "Eye in the Sky" Spencer, 54, 9842 Woodlawn Dr. Crash occurred at 7:34 a.m. Plane crashed in a parking lot at Lincoln High School. There was no fire, but firefighters remained on the scene for more than two hours. They sprayed protective, fire-retardant foam on the plane. Cause of crash not officially reported. Investigation is underway by Midcity Police and FAA agents. Results not expected for several days.

At about 9:45 a.m., wreckage loaded onto a trailer and taken to Midcity Municipal Airport for further study. Lots of "lookie-loos." Police estimate a crowd of 1,000—mostly high school students.

Spencer wasn't hurt. In fact, no injuries reported at all. Spencer has 30+ years of flying experience and has been flying for KMOR for five years. In fact, he was an "ace" during the Vietnam conflict. He flew traffic patrols for local radio station KCHR for 9 years as the "King of Traffic."

"The engine started making funny sounds and then just died," Spencer claims. "I tried to land it, but I lost control and the thing just fell like a rock. I'm just glad I came out okay and came down in a parking lot rather than on top a house or a school building. I've had a few close calls in my day, but I was never more afraid than I was today."

Cliff Albert, KMOR news director, said "Traffic Watch" will be back on the air tomorrow morning. Station will lease a plane from Allied Aviation.

"I plan to be back in the air tomorrow morning," Spencer announced. "If you fall off a horse, you gotta get right back on, right?"

SHOT LIST:
1. Cover shot—crash scene with police, fire trucks and plane   :06
2. Close-up shot—Spencer   :08
3. Medium shot—plane wreckage   :06
4. Cover shot—crowd of people   :06
5. Medium shot—plane being loaded onto trailer   :07
                                                    TOTAL   :33

● TV STUDIO PACKAGE (VO/SOT) 1

Write a VO/SOT in correct KCTI news style from the following information. Include an on-camera introduction and tail. (TRT 1:00)

All information obtained from Midcity Antique Automobile Lovers Association (MAALA) spokesperson Jeffrey W. Ryan.

Big antique car auction last night. '29 Duesenberg brought $175,000. It was a Model J, owned by Sara M. Flint (Los Angeles). It was bought by Randolph T. Harris (Denver). It was the 5th highest price in history paid for a car at a public auction. Auction was part of National Association of Antique and Classic Car Clubs of North America Convention. Convention being held at the "Town and Country Hotel" in Midcity, 7546 Valley Center Parkway. Auction held in hotel's "Monarch Room." Auction conducted by Waylon J. Ramsey, 51, of Auto Auction Authorities.

More than $3,750,000 bid at auction. 62 cars sold in all. 550 certified bidders from every state in the U.S., plus bidders from Canada and Mexico. Approximately 2,500 persons watched auction from the gallery.

Second highest price of the night was for a '34 Duesenberg. M.T. Terpin (Des Moines) sold it to Warren L. Kenning (Dallas) for $128,000.

Bargain of the night was a '49 VW Beetle. It sold for only $5,250. Seller was Conchita T. Martinez (Miami). Buyer was Mary A. Odendahl (St. Louis).

Bidding was spirited and intense for most of the night. Lots of long bidding wars. Auction lasted until 1:50 a.m. this morning.

No Midcity buyers or sellers. Convention ends tomorrow. Cars on display and open to public from 10:00 a.m.-10:00 p.m. Admission is $5.00 for adults and $2.50 for children under 12.

SHOT LIST:
1. Cover shot—cars, bidders, audience		:06
2. Medium shot—'29 Dusie with old/new owners		:04
3. Close-up shot—Harris		:04
4. Medium shot—audience		:04
5. Cover shot—bidders		:04
6. Medium shot—auctioneer		:04
7. Medium shot—Ryan		:04
8. SOT—Ryan		:07
9. Medium shot—'49 VW with old/new owners		:08
	TOTAL	:45

RYAN SOT:
"The bidding was a bit rich for any of our members and we didn't have anyone who wanted to part with a car. It was great fun, though. These cars are fabulous."

• TV STUDIO PACKAGE (VO/SOT) 2

Write a VO/SOT in correct KCTI news style from the following information. Include an on-camera introduction and tail. (TRT :40)

Accident at Midcity Municipal Airport at 8:35 a.m. this morning. Two local men knocked to the ground by a runaway vintage airplane. The two men were pulled to safety as the aircraft ran wildly in an elliptical pattern for fifteen minutes.

William G. Vernon, 54, the owner of the plane, and Robert B. Knox, 39, were working on the engine of the Ryan PT-22 trainer when the airplane jumped the wheel blocks and began to spin in an "erratic" fashion, according to witnesses. The plane posed a serious hazard until it crashed into a twin-engine Bonanza plane near the hangar section, according to Richard T. Allen, airport operations manager.

Vernon and Knox were knocked to the airstrip tarmac when they attempted to halt the aircraft and both were stunned and semiconscious as the plane whirled in an unpredictable pattern. Pilots and mechanics at the airport pulled the two men from the path of the unmanned plane.

The World War II plane finally crashed into the Bonanza, which is owned by the Tibbs Flying Service, and came to a halt, said Allen.

Vernon and Knox were transported to Midcity General Hospital and were released after receiving treatment for contusions and lacerations on their heads, arms and legs.

Both the PT-22 and the Bonanza were heavily damaged as the wooden propeller of the PT-22 ground into the side of the Bonanza and came to a halt.

SHOT LIST:
1. Cover shot—planes hooked together and people :06
2. Medium shot—Vernon and Knox being treated :08
3. Close-up shot—propeller stuck in plane :04
4. Medium shot—Allen :04
5. Allen SOT :04
6. Cover shot—workers trying to separate planes :07
                                                                    TOTAL :33

ALLEN SOT:
"It was a freak accident, but those two guys were very lucky that so many people were around to pull them to safety."

● TV STUDIO PACKAGE (VO/SOT) 3

Write a VO/SOT in correct KCTI news style from the following information. Include an on-camera introduction and tail. (TRT 1:00)

Two West Midcity men are raising buffalo on their 80-acre ranch. They released their herd to the open pasture today for the first time.

L. Theodore "Ted" McFadden and John R. "Jack" Willis bought the buffalo, 30 head, in South Dakota. They paid $60,000 for the herd.

Raising buffalo is better for several reasons, according to Jack Willis:

(1) Buffalo eat weeds and scrub brush that cattle won't touch.
(2) Buffalo are heartier and so can withstand cold and heat better.
(3) Buffalo have more meat on them than cattle do.
(4) Buffalo meat has less fat than beef from cattle.
(5) Buffalo meat tastes better than beef from cattle.

Raising buffalo has some drawbacks, according to Ted McFadden:

(1) Buffalo are harder to handle than cattle. They're more temperamental and excitable.
(2) Buffalo need stronger fences, because they're stronger than cattle.
(3) Buffalo meat is more expensive than beef from cattle. It's at least 58¢ per pound more on all cuts.

The men plan to sell their buffalo meat to restaurants in Midcity. They have no plans to sell to retail stores or markets or to private individuals.

SHOT LIST:
1. Cover shot—buffalo in pasture		:06
2. Medium shot—men talking		:04
3. Close-up shot—Jack Willis		:08
4. SOT—Willis		:06
5. Medium shot—buffalo eating grass		:04
6. Close-up shot—Ted McFadden		:08
7. SOT—McFadden		:06
8. Close-up shot—head of a buffalo looking at camera		:04
9. Cover shot—buffalo moving around in pasture		:07
	TOTAL	:53

WILLIS SOT:
"We really think the market for buffalo meat is ready to explode. It's a sweeter meat. It tastes great and it's a lot better for you."

McFADDEN SOT:
"We're hoping people will be willing to pay a little extra for higher quality, better-tasting meat. It's a gamble, though. A big one."

• TV STUDIO PACKAGE (VO/SOT) 4

Write a VO/SOT in correct KCTI news style from the following information. Include an on-camera introduction and tail. (TRT 1:00)

Big fire at a Rexall's drugstore last night at 790 Main St. (West Midcity). Nancy D. Waldrip, 44, is the manager. Stores on either side of Rexall's, Pro Image Sports, and Jake's Bar & Grill are open for business as usual. All the stores in the strip mall are approximately 8 years old.

Fire started 11:00 p.m. Fire burned until 3:00 a.m. Firefighters stayed on scene until 11:00 a.m. this morning for mop-up activities. Most of the damage in the warehouse portion of the store. Retail area suffered mostly smoke and water damage. Fire essentially contained in the warehouse area. Some actual fire damage done to the pharmacy. Pharmacy is right next to the warehouse area.

One person killed in fire. Bernard V. Chang, 27, 568 Orange Ave., a security guard for Rodger's Police Patrol, was found dead near the rear entrance to Rexall's. An autopsy is pending, but police speculate he died from smoke inhalation.

This is the 3rd fire at a Rexall's drug store in Midcity in the last two months. The first store hit was on Avocado Blvd. (North Midcity) and the 2nd was on Fletcher Parkway (South Midcity), across from the "South City Shopping Plaza." Both earlier fires started in the warehouse areas, too.

Midcity Fire Capt. Linda M. Smith estimated damage from last night's fire at $1,750,000. She suspects arson in all three Rexall's fires.

SHOT LIST:

1. Cover shot—flames and firefighter activity	:06
2. Medium shot—covered body	:06
3. Medium shot—Waldrip	:04
4. SOT—Waldrip	:09
5. Cover shot—warehouse area	:08
6. Medium shot—Smith	:04
7. SOT—Smith	:09
8. Cover shot—mopping-up by firefighters	:07
TOTAL	:53

WALDRIP SOT:
"It'll take us a couple of days to get the place cleaned up, but we should be open for business sometime next week. Our warehouse area is totally destroyed, but we can bring in some large overseas shipping containers to use until we can rebuild."

SMITH SOT:
"We found several gasoline-soaked rags under some bushes near the store and there were signs of forced entry. There's no doubt in my mind that this fire was deliberately set. The other two fires were started in the same way."

● TV SOUNDBITE 1

Write an introduction and tail in correct KCTI news style from the following information for the soundbite.
(TRT :20)

Last night somebody stole an Apple computer from Midcity University's Computer Instructional Laboratory located in MacMillan Hall. Value of unit set at $5,500. Neither Midcity University Police officers nor Midcity Police officers have any leads at the present time.

Lawrence W. Matthews, dir. of computer facilities at MU, reported the room, which housed 13 computer terminals, was locked, but the locks had been broken.

The computer was used to help acquaint students with a variety of word-processing programs and desktop publishing techniques.

MATTHEWS SOT: (TRT :10)
"The sad thing is we probably won't be able to replace the unit this year. We're going to install better locks, though, and we're adding an alarm system, too. This isn't going to happen to us again."

● TV SOUNDBITE 2

Write an introduction and tail in correct KCTI news style from the following information for the soundbite.
(TRT :20)

State Senator Lester L. Murakami (D-Midcity) is a happy man today. His bill to provide $850,000 for a new park in Midcity was signed by Gov. Sorenson this morning.

Construction at the East Midcity site—corner of Jackson Dr. and Daffodil Rd.—should begin early next month, according to Murakami. Construction estimated to take three months, Murakami stated.

Murakami is up for re-election this year. He is running against lawyer Lucille M. Edwards, a Republican.

The 15-acre park will feature 2 softball diamonds (both lighted), a children's playground, BBQs, picnic tables, a jogging track and restrooms.

MURAKAMI SOT: (TIME :08)
"I'm very happy. We need that park. It took a little bit of lobbying on my part, but it was worth it. I hope the park will be only the beginning of the revitalization process for East Midcity."

- ## TV SOUNDBITE 3

Write an introduction and tail in correct KCTI news style from the following information for the soundbite.
(TRT :30)

Unemployment is up in Midcity for the 7th straight month. Rate climbed to 6.7% of the work force last month. The month before it was 6.3%. About 49,200 men and women out of work last month compared to 46,800 the month before. Last year for the same month, the jobless rate was 5.5%.

Midcity Chamber of Commerce is going to hold a news conference tomorrow to discuss ways to combat the growing unemployment.

According to Billie Jean Miller, pres. of the Midcity Chamber of Commerce, the Midcity C of C will provide details associated with two major proposals:

(1) Lobby state legislature to reduce the minimum wage to $4.00 per hour.
(2) Launch a nationwide advertising campaign in an effort to attract new businesses to Midcity.

MILLER SOT: (TIME :12)
    "The job situation in Midcity is pretty bad right now and it could get worse. There just aren't enough jobs to go around and with money getting tighter, the job situation could get even uglier. We're hoping to try a couple of things that might stimulate the economy."

- ## TV SOUNDBITE 4

Write an introduction and tail in correct KCTI news style from the following information for the soundbite.
(TRT :30)

A local man is dead after an early morning confrontation with Midcity police officers. The officers, responding to a domestic violence call at 4:30 a.m., shot and killed the man outside a South Midcity residence. Police stated a toy gun was recovered at the scene, but initial details are sketchy. The shooting took place at a single-family home at 361 Texas St. Officials are awaiting the completion of ballistic tests to determine who fired the fatal shot. Officers Lynda R. Stein, 28, and Carlos D. Vega, 25, approached the man who was standing on the porch of the residence, according to David M. Cohen, MPD spokesperson. The name of the victim has not been released pending notification of next of kin.

COHEN SOT: (TIME :10)
    "As the officers approached the man, he pointed what appeared to be a weapon of some sort at the officers. When he refused to drop his weapon, both officers fired. The victim was struck once in the chest. The officers tried to resuscitate the man, but he died at the scene."

● TV REPORTER PACKAGE 1

Write an introduction and tail in correct KCTI news style from the following information for the reporter package. (TRT 1:00)

Local garbage workers began their strike today. Picketers out in force this morning in front of the Dept. of Sanitation garage.

Brief confrontation between workers and management personnel who attempted to cross picket line. No injuries. Just a lot of pushing and name calling.

No negotiation session scheduled for today, but a session is set for tomorrow at 8:00 a.m.

Workers want a pay hike of 8%, but the Midcity Board of Supervisors has offered just 3%. The average garbage worker earns $27,500.

Jill Liang covered the story for KCTI. She closes story with a stand-up. Picketers are seen behind her.

LIANG PACKAGE IN:

"The picketers were all from Public Employees Local 3-4-5."

LIANG PACKAGE OUT:

"Liang for KCTI News."

LIANG PACKAGE TIME: :46

● TV REPORTER PACKAGE 2

Write an introduction and tail in correct KCTI news style from the following information for the reporter package. (TRT 1:00)

More bad news on the housing front. The average price for a single-family home in Midcity is now $189,000, according to the Midcity Realtors Association. Last year at this time the average price was $177,000.

The high cost has put a dent in the local real estate business. Sales on single-family homes are down 35% from just six months ago and are down 50% from a year ago.

KCTI reporter Mollie Smith covered the story. She and her husband, Gary, bought a new home two weeks ago. She filed the report from a new housing project construction site. She opens the report sitting on a backhoe machine with construction activity going on behind her.

SMITH PACKAGE IN:

"A lot of Midcity residents are being priced right out of the single-family housing market these days."

SMITH PACKAGE OUT:

"Mollie Smith, KCTI News, West Midcity."

SMITH PACKAGE TIME: :42

• TV REPORTER PACKAGE 3

Write an introduction and tail in correct KCTI news style from the following information for the reporter package. (TRT 1:30)

Attendance at Midcity Zoo is up from last year. Latest figures show 1,500,000 persons have visited the zoo so far this year, compared to 1,300,000 persons at this time last year.

All of the different and exotic animals are the major attractions, but KCTI reporter Kevin Cooney has done a story about another part of the zoo. He found out that there are over 200,000 different varieties of plants and flowers at the zoo. Some are extremely rare and valuable. In fact, the plants and flowers at the zoo are worth more than the animals. The animals are worth about $8,700,000 and the plants and flowers about $8,750,000, according to zoo officials. There are 16,120 animals at the zoo.

Cooney begins his report standing in front of the zoo entrance.

COONEY PACKAGE IN:

"You can find crowds like this every day here at the Midcity Zoo."

COONEY PACKAGE OUT:

"From the Midcity Zoo, I'm Kevin Cooney for KCTI News."

COONEY PACKAGE TIME: 1:08

● TV REPORTER PACKAGE 4

Write an introduction and tail in correct KCTI news style from the following information for the reporter package. (TRT 1:30)

Midcity Police are worried about a new weapon called a "Potato Gun." It is cheap, accessible and it is sweeping the country, according to a nationwide survey of law enforcement officials.

Most potato guns resemble shoulder-held missile launchers. A potato is used as the projectile. Most potato guns are homemade or readily available at local swap meets and flea markets.

The guns are built from plastic pipe tubes (PVC pipe). Potatoes are jammed down one end of the tube and the weapon is fired by igniting some type of flammable substance, such as aerosol hair spray or lighter fluid, in a container attached to the opposite end of the tube.

Midcity Police spokesman David M. Cohen reports tests have shown that potatoes launched from potato guns can travel at speeds of up to 500-600 feet per second and have dented car doors and smashed windows.

So far, no potato gun-related deaths have been reported, but Cohen says it's just a matter of time unless something is done to ban or regulate the guns. The Midcity Board of Supervisors is scheduled to discuss the issue of regulating potato guns at its next meeting.

KCTI reporter Tim Ramirez has a story about potato guns in Midcity. He talked with police officers, witnessed a demonstration of what potato guns can do and visited a local swap meet where potato guns are the "hot" item. He closes his story with a stand-up at the swap meet. He is holding a potato gun.

RAMIREZ PACKAGE IN:

"This dent was made by a potato."

RAMIREZ PACKAGE OUT:

"From the North City Swap Meet, I'm Tim Ramirez for KCTI News."

RAMIREZ PACKAGE TIME: 1:00

● TV LIVE SHOT 1

Write an introduction in correct KCTI news style from the following information for the live report. (TRT 1:30)

Reporter Susan Trang is live at the Midcity Municipal Airport. A computer failure has shut down the airport. No flights have taken off or landed for more than 60 minutes. Airport officials are working on the problem and they expect to have the problem corrected within an hour.

Lots of congestion at the airport. Today is traditionally one of the busiest of the year at the airport. Lines are long. Tempers are short. As a peace offering, Trans-Continental Airlines has announced it will offer inconvenienced ticketed passengers a half-price travel coupon that will be good for any Trans-Continental flight for one year. Other airlines are expected to follow suit.

Trang will begin her report from in front of one of the ticket counters. She will update the situation and interview an airport official.

Trang's report will run 1:15, so the introduction should run :15.

● TV LIVE SHOT 2

Write an introduction in correct KCTI news style from the following information for the live shot. (TRT 1:30)

Reporter Ricardo Rivera is live at the scene of a hostage situation. Reportedly, according to Midcity Police, a man is holding his wife and three children hostage in their rented house at 819 Dallas Rd. in East Midcity. The man has a gun and has fired at least one shot at police officers, police say. Details are sketchy, but neighbors say the man, Douglas S. Robinson, 31, often had loud arguments with his wife. He recently lost his job at General Aeronautics and has been seen sitting on his porch drinking beer and hard liquor almost every day for hours at a time for the past week.

Rhonda L. Robinson, 29, and her children, ages 3, 5, 8, have been sighted in the house. They apparently have not been injured. Police have had no direct communication with anyone in the house, but they are trying to establish a phone line connection with Robinson.

Rivera will begin his report near the house and behind the police line.

Rivera's report will run 1:15, so the introduction should run :15.

● TV LIVE SHOT 3

Write an introduction in correct KCTI news style from the following information for the live shot. (TRT 1:30)

Reporter Ken Warren is live at the Midcity CityFest. It's a 3-day festival of music, food and handicrafts in the downtown area. Approximately 8 square blocks of the downtown area are cordoned off. More than 50 musical groups—some local, but others are nationally and internationally known—are scheduled to perform on 10 different stages placed strategically around the area. Music will include jazz, rock, blues, folk, gospel, country-western and many more. Most of the big restaurants and specialty-food establishments in the city have booths. More than 300 artists and handcrafters have booths, too. More than 55,000 people are expected to attend over the three days. This is the 5th annual CityFest.

Warren will begin his report right in front of one of the music stages. He'll then wander around a bit pointing out some of the other attractions.

Warren's report will run 1:10, so the introduction should run :20.

● TV LIVE SHOT 4

Write an introduction in correct KCTI news style from the following information for the live shot. (TRT 1:30)

Reporter Lori Lynn is live at the scene of a display by the Midcity Police Department. Police Chief Harold L. Kettner is hoping to convince the Board of Supervisors that erecting surplus military tents on the grounds of the Midcity County Jail for shoplifters and other petty thieves will help ease overcrowding at the jail. The chief has erected 4 tents for display purposes. The chief believes the tent jail is the best cost-saving method for housing up to 100 petty criminals, so scarce indoor jail space can be used to house more violent inmates. The chief estimates the cost of the tent jail to be $5 per inmate. The cost of the typical bed space in concrete jails is $50,000 per inmate. The Supervisors are scheduled to vote on the chief's proposal next week.

Lynn will begin her report inside one of the large tents. She'll talk about some of the tent's features and then go outside to tour the grounds and talk to Chief Kettner.

Lynn's report will run 1:10, so the introduction should run :20.

Pronunciation Guide

Use the following pronouncers for names included in this workbook.

Beeman, Theodore N. (THEE-uh-dohr BEE-muhn)
Bleyer, William B. (BLEYE-er)
Bohanen, Ruth D. (Boh-HAN-nehn)
Bott, Jason A. (Baht)
Castro, Maria E. (KAS-troh)
Chaney, Darlene A. (CHAY-nee)
Chen, Lawrence C. (Chehn)
Chu, Brenda L. (Choo)
Chu, Franklin R. (Choo)
Cohen, David M. (COH-ehn)
Curlee, Linda Rae (KER-lee)
Detonio, Sylvanie (SIHL-vah-nee Day-TOH-nee-oh)
Dozier, David D. (DOHZ-zher)
Draper, Brett (DRAY-per)
Eggers, Virginia W. (EHG-gers)
Epperlein, James H. (EHP-per-leyen)
Estrada, Sharon (Ehs-STRAH-duh)
Frazier, Lowell F. (FRAY-zher)
Gandolf, Allison F. (GAN-dawlf)
Garcia, Grace (Gahr-SEE-uh)
Guerrero, Jorge E. (HOHR-gay Guh-RAIR-roh)
Gunnersley, Craig H. (GUHN-ners-lee)
Gwynn, Tony (Gwihn)
Heath, Carl A. (Heeth)
Hisaka, Lloyd K. (Hee-SAHK-kuh)
Holtzman, Nancy C. (HOHLTZ-muhn)
Howatt, William D. (HOW-wuht)
Huston, Wilma E. (HEW-stuhn)
Hyde, Walter N. (Heyed)
Ishida, Sharon A. (Ish-SHEE-duh)
Kaiser, Edward K. (KEYE-zer)
Kalakaua, Roscoe H. (KAH-lah-kah-wah)
Kamau, Bradley J. (Kuh-MOW)
Keever, Jane T. (KEE-ver)
Kegel, Craig G. (KAY-guhl)
Kiperts, Donald K. (KIHP-perts)
Kiperts, Jane V. (KIHP-perts)

Kleinehorst, Carolyn C. (KLEYEN-hohrst)
Krumm, Martin C. (Kruhm)
Lauzen, Martha B. (LAH-zuhn)
Leitner, Laurie (LEYET-ner)
Liang, Jill (LEE-ang)
Lo-chi, Wang (LOH-chee)
Lopez, David E. (LOH-pehz)
Lopez, Juan R. (Wahn LOH-pehz)
Lopez, Maria Y. (LOH-pehz)
Loren, Donna Z. (LOHR-rehn)
Lowe, Barbara B. (Loh)
Lowe, Paul J. (Loh)
Lowenstein, Lydia (LIH-dee-uh LOH-ehn-steyen)
Luter, John A. (LOO-ter)
Macias, Jorge T. (HOHR-gay Muh-SEE-uhs)
Marlow, John B. (MAHR-loh)
Martinez, Conchita T. (Kahn-CHEE-tuh Mahr-TEEN-ehz)
McTighe, Michelle V. (Mihk-TEYE)
Morren, Ronald S. (MOHR-rehn)
Mueller, Barbara M. (MEWL-ler)
Muller, David D. (MUHL-ler)
Muller, Marvin (MUHL-ler)
Murakami, Lester L. (MER-uh-kah-mee)
Nater, Pamela T. (NAY-ter)
Noriega, Christina (NOHR-ee-ay-guh)
Odendahl, Mary A. (OH-dehn-dahl)
Otterman, Eric A. (AHT-ter-muhn)
Perez, Jerry F. (PER-rehz)
Ramirez, Tim (RAH-mihr-rehz)
Ramos, Miguel (Mee-GEHL RAY-mohs)
Ramos, Ricardo E. (Ree-CAHR-doh RAY-mohs)
Ramos, Thomas P. (RAY-mohs)
Reeger, Jane A. (REE-ger)
Rivera, Ricardo (REE-cahr-doh Ruh-VIHR-uh)
Rodriguez, Enrique C. (Ehn-REE-kay RAHD-ree-gehz)
Rodriquez, Melissa J. (RAHD-ree-gehz)
Romero, Rita R. (Roh-MAIR-oh)

Rosario, Katrina P. (Roh-SAHR-ee-oh)
Sakamoto, Gloria C. (SAHK-kah-moh-toh)
Sanchez, Maria A. (SAN-chehz)
Sandoval, Carmen F. (SAN-doh-vahl)
Saxon, John S. (SAX-suhn)
Schroeder, Robert J. (SCHROH-der)
Seinfeld, Helen K. (SEYEN-fehld)
Shippen, Terrence P. (SHIHP-pehn)
Spadoro, George (Spah-DOHR-oh)
Stein, Lynda R. (Steyen)
Stein, Rachael W. (Steyen)
Taite, William W. (Tayt)
Tanibe, Patricia I. (Tuh-NEE-bee)
Tennessen, Sheryl (TEHN-nehs-sehn)

Tippler, Sarah Jane (TIHP-pler)
Torgerson, John J. (TOHR-ger-suhn)
Torres, Raul J. (RAH-ool TOHR-rehz)
Tupperman, Norman L. (TUHP-per-muhn)
Tybo, Ruby M. (TEYE-boh)
Valdez, Mark (VAHL-dehz)
Vance, Eve Bayani (BEYE-yahn-nee)
Vargas, Marilyn D. (VAHR-guhs)
Vega, Carlos D. (VAY-guh)
Villa, Elena L (VEE-yuh)
Voltrov, Alexi Z. (VOHL-trawf)
Waxton, Marc P. (WAX-tuhn)
Wong, Jennifer (Wawng)
Zavesky, Matthew (Zuh-VEHS-kee)

Learning Opportunities

● **LEARNING OPPORTUNITY 1**

Tape record 30 minutes of an "all-news" radio station's programming or a "news/talk" radio station's programming starting at the top of the hour during morning drive-time (6:00 a.m.-9:00 a.m.).

Play the tape and list the stories in chronological order. Note which stories are readers, readers with actualities, reporter voicers and reporter wraparounds.

How long is each story? List the strengths and weaknesses of the writing for each story.

Was the copy clear, understandable and interesting? Why or why not? Rate the conversationality of the copy.

What improvements would you suggest? Why? (Use the appropriate logging sheet in Appendix 3. Make a photocopy of the logging sheet in case you need it.)

● **LEARNING OPPORTUNITY 2**

Tape record a morning newscast on five different radio stations. Try to pick stations with different programming formats—album-oriented rock, jazz, classic rock, country and western, urban contemporary, adult contemporary, etc.

As you listen to the taped newscasts, list the stories in chronological order. Note which stories are readers, readers with actualities, reporter voicers and reporter wraparounds. Note the length of each story. List the strengths and weaknesses of the writing for each story. Rate the conversationality of the copy.

What improvements would you suggest? Why? What differences do you detect among the stations? Why do you think the differences exist? (Use the appropriate logging sheet in Appendix 3. You'll probably need four photocopies of the logging sheet.)

● **LEARNING OPPORTUNITY 3**

Tape record an early morning newscast and a late afternoon newscast on the same radio station. As you listen to the taped newscasts, list the stories in chronological order. Note which stories are readers, readers with actualities, reporter voicers and reporter wraparounds. Note the length of each story. List the strengths and weaknesses of the writing for each story. Rate the conversationality of the copy.

What improvements would you suggest? Why? What differences do you detect between the two newscasts? Why do you think the differences exist? (Use the appropriate logging sheet in Appendix 3. You'll probably need a photocopy of the logging sheet.)

● LEARNING OPPORTUNITY 4

Tape record a network newscast and a local newscast on the same radio station. As you listen to the taped newscasts, list the stories in chronological order. Note which stories are readers, readers with actualities, reporter voicers and reporter wraparounds. Note the length of each story.

List the strengths and weaknesses of the writing for each story. Rate the conversationality of the copy.

What improvements would you suggest? Why? What differences do you detect between the two newscasts? Why do you think the differences exist? (Use the appropriate logging sheet in Appendix 3. You'll probably need a photocopy of the logging sheet.)

● LEARNING OPPORTUNITY 5

Tape record a total of 30 minutes of radio news on your favorite station. If you can, tape at least two newscasts in the early morning, two in the afternoon and two in the evening.

As you listen to the tape, list the stories in chronological order. Note which stories are readers, readers with actualities, reporter voicers and reporter wraparounds. Note the length of each story. Rate the conversationality of the copy.

List the strengths and weaknesses of the writing for each story. What improvements would you suggest? Why?

Did you find much repetition? Were the leads different when a story aired more than once? In what other ways were similar stories aired on different newscasts made to sound different? (Use the appropriate logging sheet in Appendix 3. You'll probably need five photocopies of the logging sheet.)

● LEARNING OPPORTUNITY 6

This is a two-step learning opportunity.

(1) Tape record a total of 30 minutes of radio news on your favorite station. If you can, tape at least two newscasts in the early morning, two in the afternoon and two in the evening. As you listen to the tape, list the stories in chronological order. Note the length of each story. Rate the conversationality of the copy. List the strengths and weaknesses of the writing for each story. What improvements would you suggest? Why?

(2) Scan the morning newspaper for the same day you recorded your radio newscasts. Look for the same stories you heard on the radio. List the strengths and weaknesses of the writing for each story.

Scan the morning newspaper for the day after you recorded your radio newscasts. Look for the same stories you heard on the radio. List the strengths and weaknesses of the writing for each story.

How do the writing styles of the newspaper and the radio station compare? List similarities and differences. Compare the reporting. What did the radio stories leave out that was included in the newspaper stories? What did the radio stories include that was not in the newspaper stories? (Use the appropriate logging sheets in Appendix 3.) You'll probably need five photocopies of the logging sheet for the radio newscasts and three photocopies of the logging sheet for the newspaper stories.)

● LEARNING OPPORTUNITY 7

Tape record a 30-minute local TV newscast. Play the tape and list the stories in chronological order. Note which stories are readers, readers with graphics, soundbites, VOs, VO/SOTs, reporter packages and live shots. Note the length of each story.

Rate the conversationality of each story. List the strengths and weaknesses of the writing in each story. What improvements would you suggest? Why? (Use the appropriate logging sheet in Appendix 3. You'll probably need a photocopy of the logging sheet.)

- ## LEARNING OPPORTUNITY 8

   Tape record an early evening local TV newscast and a late night local TV newscast on the same station. Play the tapes and list the stories in chronological order. Note which stories are readers, readers with graphics, soundbites, VOs, VO/SOTs, reporter packages and live shots. Note the length of each story.

   Rate the conversationality of each story. List the strengths and weaknesses of the writing in each story. What improvements would you suggest? Why?

   What differences do you detect between the two newscasts? How were repeated stories made to sound different? (Use the appropriate logging sheet in Appendix 3. You'll probably need two photocopies of the logging sheet.)

- ## LEARNING OPPORTUNITY 9

   Tape record an early evening local TV newscast on two different stations. Play the tapes and list the stories in chronological order. Note which stories are readers, readers with graphics, soundbites, VOs, VO/SOTs, reporter packages and live shots. Note the length of each story. Rate the conversationality of each story. List the strengths and weaknesses of the writing in each story. What improvements would you suggest? Why?

   What differences do you detect between the two stations? Which newscast do you prefer? Why? (Use the appropriate logging sheet in Appendix 3. You'll probably need three photocopies of the logging sheet.)

- ## LEARNING OPPORTUNITY 10

   Tape record a network TV newscast. Play the tape and list the stories in chronological order. Note which stories are readers, readers with graphics, soundbites, VOs, VO/SOTs, reporter packages and live shots. Note the length of each story.

   Rate the conversationality of each story. List the strengths and weaknesses of the writing in each story. What improvements would you suggest? Why? (Use the appropriate logging sheet in Appendix 3. You'll probably need a photocopy of the logging sheet.)

- ## LEARNING OPPORTUNITY 11

   Tape record a network TV newscast and a late night local TV newscast on the same station and on the same day. Play the tapes and list the stories in chronological order. Note which stories are readers, readers with graphics, soundbites, VOs, VO/SOTs, reporter packages and live shots. Note the length of each story.

   Rate the conversationality of each story. List the strengths and weaknesses of the writing in each story. What improvements would you suggest? Why?

   What differences do you detect between the two newscasts? Were any stories included in both newscasts? If so, how were they different? (Use the appropriate logging sheet in Appendix 3. You'll probably need three photocopies of the logging sheet.)

- ## LEARNING OPPORTUNITY 12

   This is a two-step learning opportunity.

   (1) Tape record a late night TV newscast on your favorite station. Play the tape and list the stories in chronological order. Note the length of each story. Rate the conversationality of the copy. List the strengths and weaknesses of the writing for each story. What improvements would you suggest? Why?

   (2) Scan the morning newspaper for the same day you recorded your TV newscast. Look for the same stories

you saw on TV. List the strengths and weaknesses of the writing for each story.

Scan the morning newspaper for the day after you recorded your TV newscast. Look for the same stories you saw on TV. List the strengths and weaknesses of the writing for each story.

How do the writing styles of the newspaper and the TV station compare? List similarities and differences. Compare the reporting. What did the TV stories leave out that was included in the newspaper stories? What did the TV stories include that was not in the newspaper stories? (Use the appropriate logging sheets in Appendix 3. You'll probably need a photocopy of each of the logging sheets.)

Logging Sheets

Logging Sheet: Learning Opportunity 1
All-News Radio Newscast

NAME: _____

DATE: _____ STATION: _____

Story	Story Type	Length	Conversational	Strong/Weak	Improvements
1.					
2.					
3.					
4.					
5.					
6.					
7.					
8.					
9.					
10.					
11.					
12.					
13.					
14.					
15.					

COMMENTS: _____

_____

_____

_____

_____

_____

Logging Sheet: Learning Opportunity 2
Morning Radio Newscasts

NAME: _____

DATE: _____ STATION: _____

Story	Story Type	Length	Conversational	Strong/Weak	Improvements
1.					
2.					
3.					
4.					
5.					
6.					
7.					
8.					
9.					
10.					
11.					
12.					
13.					
14.					
15.					

COMMENTS: _____

_____

_____

_____

_____

_____

_____

Logging Sheet: Learning Opportunity 3
Morning/Afternoon Radio Newscasts

NAME: _____

DATE: _____ STATION: _____

Story	Story Type	Length	Conversational	Strong/Weak	Improvements
1.					
2.					
3.					
4.					
5.					
6.					
7.					
8.					
9.					
10.					
11.					
12.					
13.					
14.					
15.					

COMMENTS: _____

_____

_____

_____

_____

_____

Logging Sheet: Learning Opportunity 4
Network/Local Radio Newscasts

NAME: _____

DATE: _____ STATION: _____

Story	Story Type	Length	Conversational	Strong/Weak	Improvements
1. _____					_____
2. _____					_____
3. _____					_____
4. _____					_____
5. _____					_____
6. _____					_____
7. _____					_____
8. _____					_____
9. _____					_____
10. _____					_____
11. _____					_____
12. _____					_____
13. _____					_____
14. _____					_____
15. _____					_____

COMMENTS: _____

_____

_____

_____

_____

_____

Logging Sheet: Learning Opportunity 5
A Day of Radio Newscasts

NAME: _____

DATE: _____ STATION: _____

Story	Story Type	Length	Conversational	Strong/Weak	Improvements
1.					
2.					
3.					
4.					
5.					
6.					
7.					
8.					
9.					
10.					
11.					
12.					
13.					
14.					
15.					

COMMENTS: _____

_____

_____

_____

_____

_____

Logging Sheet: Learning Opportunity 6
Radio Newscast vs. Newspaper Stories

NAME: _____

DATE: _____ STATION: _____

Story	Story Type	Length	Conversational	Strong/Weak	Improvements
1.					
2.					
3.					
4.					
5.					
6.					
7.					
8.					
9.					
10.					
11.					
12.					
13.					
14.					
15.					

COMMENTS: _____

_____

_____

_____

_____

_____

Logging Sheet: Learning Opportunity 6
Radio Newscast vs. Newspaper Stories

NAME: _____

DATE: _____ NEWSPAPER: _____

Story	Strengths	Weaknesses
1.		
2.		
3.		
4.		
5.		
6.		
7.		
8.		
9.		
10.		
11.		
12.		
13.		
14.		
15.		

COMMENTS: _____

_____

_____

_____

_____

_____

Logging Sheet: Learning Opportunity 7
TV Newscast

NAME: _____

DATE: _____ STATION: _____

Story	Story Type	Length	Conversational	Strong/Weak	Improvements
1.					
2.					
3.					
4.					
5.					
6.					
7.					
8.					
9.					
10.					
11.					
12.					
13.					
14.					
15.					

COMMENTS: _____

_____

_____

_____

_____

Logging Sheet: Learning Opportunity 8
Evening/Late Night Television Newscasts

NAME: _____

DATE: _____ STATION: _____

Story	Story Type	Length	Conversational	Strong/Weak	Improvements
1.					
2.					
3.					
4.					
5.					
6.					
7.					
8.					
9.					
10.					
11.					
12.					
13.					
14.					
15.					

COMMENTS: _____

_____

_____

_____

_____

_____

Logging Sheet: Learning Opportunity 9
Evening Television Newscasts

NAME: _____

DATE: _____ STATION: _____

Story	Story Type	Length	Conversational	Strong/Weak	Improvements
1. ___					___
2. ___					___
3. ___					___
4. ___					___
5. ___					___
6. ___					___
7. ___					___
8. ___					___
9. ___					___
10. ___					___
11. ___					___
12. ___					___
13. ___					___
14. ___					___
15. ___					___

COMMENTS: _____

_____

_____

_____

_____

_____

Logging Sheet: Learning Opportunity 10
Network Television Newscast

NAME: _____

DATE: _____ STATION: _____

Story	Story Type	Length	Conversational	Strong/Weak	Improvements
1.					
2.					
3.					
4.					
5.					
6.					
7.					
8.					
9.					
10.					
11.					
12.					
13.					
14.					
15.					

COMMENTS: _____

_____

_____

_____

_____

Logging Sheet: Learning Opportunity 11
Network/Local Television Newscasts

NAME: _____

DATE: _____ STATION: _____

Story	Story Type	Length	Conversational	Strong/Weak	Improvements
1.					
2.					
3.					
4.					
5.					
6.					
7.					
8.					
9.					
10.					
11.					
12.					
13.					
14.					
15.					

COMMENTS: _____

_____

_____

_____

_____

_____

Logging Sheet: Learning Opportunity 12
Television Newscast vs. Newspaper Stories

NAME: _____

DATE: _____ STATION: _____

Story	Story Type	Length	Conversational	Strong/Weak	Improvements
1.					
2.					
3.					
4.					
5.					
6.					
7.					
8.					
9.					
10.					
11.					
12.					
13.					
14.					
15.					

COMMENTS: _____

_____

_____

_____

_____

_____

Logging Sheet: Learning Opportunity 12
Television Newscast vs. Newspaper Stories

NAME: _____

DATE: _____ NEWSPAPER: _____

Story	Strengths	Weaknesses

1. _____

2. _____

3. _____

4. _____

5. _____

6. _____

7. _____

8. _____

9. _____

10. _____

11. _____

12. _____

13. _____

14. _____

15. _____

COMMENTS: _____

_____

_____

_____

_____

_____

APPENDIX 4

Suggested Readings

The following books will help you improve your radio-TV newswriting.

John R. Bittner and Denise A. Bittner, *Radio Journalism*
Edward Bliss, Jr. and James L. Hoyt, *Writing News for Broadcast*
Mervin Block, *Writing Broadcast News*
Mervin Block, *Rewriting Network News*
Mervin Block, *Broadcast Newswriting: The RTNDA Reference Guide*
E. Joseph Broussard and Jack F. Holgate, *Writing and Reporting Broadcast News*
David Keith Cohler, *Broadcast Journalism*
David Keith Cohler, *Broadcast Newswriting*
Irving Fang, *Television News, Radio News*
Daniel E. Garvey and William L. Rivers, *Newswriting for the Electronic Media*
Daniel E. Garvey and William L. Rivers, *Broadcast Writing*
Roy Gibson, *Radio and Television Reporting*
Carl Hausman, *Crafting the News for the Electronic Media*
John Hewitt, *Air Words: Writing for Broadcast News*
Robert L. Hilliard, *Writing for Radio and Television*
R. H. MacDonald, *A Broadcast News Manual of Style*
Peter E. Mayeux, *Broadcast News Writing and Reporting*
Donald W. Miles, *Broadcast News Handbook*
Robert Papper, *Broadcast News Writing Stylebook*
Frederick Shook, *Television Newswriting*
Frederick Shook and Dan Lattimore, *The Broadcast News Process*
G. Paul Smeyak, *Broadcast News Writing*
Mitchell Stephens, *Broadcast News*
J. Clark Weaver, *Broadcast Newswriting as Process*
Ted White, *Broadcast News Writing and Reporting*
Ted White, Adrian J. Meppen and Steve Young, *Broadcast News Writing, Reporting and Production*
Arthur Wimer and Dale Brix, *Workbook for Radio and TV News Editing and Writing*
K. Tim Wulfemeyer, *Beginning Broadcast Newswriting: A Self-Instructional Learning Experience*
Richard Yoakam and Charles F. Cremer, *ENG: Television News and the New Technology*
Steven Zousmer, *TV News Off-Camera*